The Department of Health and Human Services

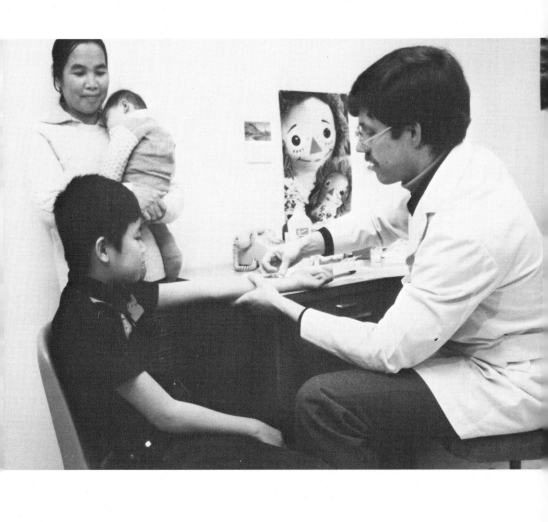

The Department of Health and Human Services

Merle Broberg

CHELSEA HOUSE PUBLISHERS

Chelsea House Publishers
Editor-in-Chief: Nancy Toff
Executive Editor: Remmel T. Nunn
Managing Editor: Karyn Gullen Browne
Copy Chief: Juliann Barbato
Picture Editor: Adrian G. Allen
Art Director: Maria Epes
Manufacturing Manager: Gerald Levine

Know Your Government
Senior Editor: Kathy Kuhtz

Staff for THE DEPARTMENT OF HEALTH AND HUMAN SERVICES
Associate Editor: Pierre Hauser
Copy Editor: Nicole Bowen
Deputy Copy Chief: Ellen Scordato
Editorial Assistant: Theodore Keyes
Picture Researcher: Dixon and Turner Research Associates
Assistant Art Director: Laurie Jewell
Senior Designer: Noreen M. Lamb
Production Coordinator: Joseph Romano

First Printing

1 3 5 7 9 8 6 4 2

Library of Congress Cataloging in Publication Data

Broberg, Merle.
    The Department of Health and Human Services / Merle Broberg.
    p.   cm. —(Know your government)
    Bibliography: p.
    Includes index.
    Surveys the history of the Department of Health and Human Services, describing its
structure, function, and influence on American society.
    ISBN 0-87754-840-4
        0-7910-0857-6 (pbk.)
    1. Human   services—United   States—History—Juvenile   literature.   2. United
States. Dept. of Health and Human Services—History—Juvenile literature.   3. Public
welfare—United States—History—Juvenile literature. [1. United States. Dept. of
Health and Human Services.   2. Human services.   3. Public welfare.]   I. Title.   II.
Series: Know your government (New York, N.Y.)   88-16213
HV91.B695 1989   CIP
353.84'2'09—dc19   AC

CONTENTS

KNOW YOUR GOVERNMENT

THE AMERICAN RED CROSS

THE BUREAU OF INDIAN AFFAIRS

THE CENTRAL INTELLIGENCE AGENCY

THE COMMISSION ON CIVIL RIGHTS

THE DEPARTMENT OF AGRICULTURE

THE DEPARTMENT OF THE AIR FORCE

THE DEPARTMENT OF THE ARMY

THE DEPARTMENT OF COMMERCE

THE DEPARTMENT OF DEFENSE

THE DEPARTMENT OF EDUCATION

THE DEPARTMENT OF ENERGY

THE DEPARTMENT OF HEALTH AND HUMAN SERVICES

THE DEPARTMENT OF HOUSING AND URBAN DEVELOPMENT

THE DEPARTMENT OF THE INTERIOR

THE DEPARTMENT OF JUSTICE

THE DEPARTMENT OF LABOR

THE DEPARTMENT OF THE NAVY

THE DEPARTMENT OF STATE

THE DEPARTMENT OF TRANSPORTATION

THE DEPARTMENT OF THE TREASURY

THE DRUG ENFORCEMENT ADMINISTRATION

THE ENVIRONMENTAL PROTECTION AGENCY

THE EQUAL EMPLOYMENT OPPORTUNITIES COMMISSION

THE FEDERAL AVIATION ADMINISTRATION

THE FEDERAL BUREAU OF INVESTIGATION

THE FEDERAL COMMUNICATIONS COMMISSION

THE FEDERAL GOVERNMENT: HOW IT WORKS

THE FEDERAL RESERVE SYSTEM

THE FEDERAL TRADE COMMISSION

THE FOOD AND DRUG ADMINISTRATION

THE FOREST SERVICE

THE HOUSE OF REPRESENTATIVES

THE IMMIGRATION AND NATURALIZATION SERVICE

THE INTERNAL REVENUE SERVICE

THE LIBRARY OF CONGRESS

THE NATIONAL AERONAUTICS AND SPACE ADMINISTRATION

THE NATIONAL ARCHIVES AND RECORDS ADMINISTRATION

THE NATIONAL FOUNDATION ON THE ARTS AND HUMANITIES

THE NATIONAL PARK SERVICE

THE NATIONAL SCIENCE FOUNDATION

THE NUCLEAR REGULATORY COMMISSION

THE PEACE CORPS

THE PRESIDENCY

THE PUBLIC HEALTH SERVICE

THE SECURITIES AND EXCHANGE COMMISSION

THE SENATE

THE SMALL BUSINESS ADMINISTRATION

THE SMITHSONIAN

THE SUPREME COURT

THE TENNESSEE VALLEY AUTHORITY

THE U.S. ARMS CONTROL AND DISARMAMENT AGENCY

THE U.S. COAST GUARD

THE U.S. CONSTITUTION

THE U.S. FISH AND WILDLIFE SERVICE

THE U.S. INFORMATION AGENCY

THE U.S. MARINE CORPS

THE U.S. MINT

THE U.S. POSTAL SERVICE

THE U.S. SECRET SERVICE

THE VETERANS ADMINISTRATION

CHELSEA HOUSE PUBLISHERS

INTRODUCTION

Government: Crises of Confidence

Arthur M. Schlesinger, jr.

From the start, Americans have regarded their government with a mixture of reliance and mistrust. The men who founded the republic did not doubt the indispensability of government. "If men were angels," observed the 51st Federalist Paper, "no government would be necessary." But men are not angels. Because human beings are subject to wicked as well as to noble impulses, government was deemed essential to assure freedom and order.

At the same time, the American revolutionaries knew that government could also become a source of injury and oppression. The men who gathered in Philadelphia in 1787 to write the Constitution therefore had two purposes in mind. They wanted to establish a strong central authority and to limit that central authority's capacity to abuse its power.

To prevent the abuse of power, the Founding Fathers wrote two basic principles into the new Constitution. The principle of federalism divided power between the state governments and the central authority. The principle of the separation of powers subdivided the central authority itself into three branches—the executive, the legislative, and the judiciary—so that "each may be a check on the other." The *Know Your Government* series focuses on the major executive departments and agencies in these branches of the federal government.

7

The Constitution did not plan the executive branch in any detail. After vesting the executive power in the president, it assumed the existence of "executive departments" without specifying what these departments should be. Congress began defining their functions in 1789 by creating the Departments of State, Treasury, and War. The secretaries in charge of these departments made up President Washington's first cabinet. Congress also provided for a legal officer, and President Washington soon invited the attorney general, as he was called, to attend cabinet meetings. As need required, Congress created more executive departments.

Setting up the cabinet was only the first step in organizing the American state. With almost no guidance from the Constitution, President Washington, seconded by Alexander Hamilton, his brilliant secretary of the treasury, equipped the infant republic with a working administrative structure. The Federalists believed in both executive energy and executive accountability and set high standards for public appointments. The Jeffersonian opposition had less faith in strong government and preferred local government to the central authority. But when Jefferson himself became president in 1801, although he set out to change the direction of policy, he found no reason to alter the framework the Federalists had erected.

By 1801 there were about 3,000 federal civilian employees in a nation of a little more than 5 million people. Growth in territory and population steadily enlarged national responsibilities. Thirty years later, when Jackson was president, there were more than 11,000 government workers in a nation of 13 million. The federal establishment was increasing at a faster rate than the population.

Jackson's presidency brought significant changes in the federal service. He believed that the executive branch contained too many officials who saw their jobs as "species of property" and as "a means of promoting individual interest." Against the idea of a permanent service based on life tenure, Jackson argued for the periodic redistribution of federal offices, contending that this was the democratic way and that official duties could be made "so plain and simple that men of intelligence may readily qualify themselves for their performance." He called this policy rotation-in-office. His opponents called it the spoils system.

In fact, partisan legend exaggerated the extent of Jackson's removals. More than 80 percent of federal officeholders retained their jobs. Jackson discharged no larger a proportion of government workers than Jefferson had done a generation earlier. But the rise in these years of mass political parties gave federal patronage new importance as a means of building the party and of rewarding activists. Jackson's successors were less restrained in the distribu-

8

tion of spoils. As the federal establishment grew—to nearly 40,000 by 1861—
the politicization of the public service excited increasing concern.

After the Civil War the spoils system became a major political issue.
High-minded men condemned it as the root of all political evil. The spoilsmen,
said the British commentator James Bryce, "have distorted and depraved the
mechanism of politics." Patronage, by giving jobs to unqualified, incompetent,
and dishonest persons, lowered the standards of public service and nourished
corrupt political machines. Office-seekers pursued presidents and cabinet
secretaries without mercy. "Patronage," said Ulysses S. Grant after his
presidency, "is the bane of the presidential office." "Every time I appoint
someone to office," said another political leader, "I make a hundred enemies
and one ingrate." George William Curtis, the president of the National Civil
Service Reform League, summed up the indictment. He said,

> The theory which perverts public trusts into party spoils, making public
> employment dependent upon personal favor and not on proved merit,
> necessarily ruins the self-respect of public employees, destroys the
> function of party in a republic, prostitutes elections into a desperate
> strife for personal profit, and degrades the national character by lower-
> ing the moral tone and standard of the country.

The object of civil service reform was to promote efficiency and honesty in
the public service and to bring about the ethical regeneration of public life. Over
bitter opposition from politicians, the reformers in 1883 passed the Pendleton
Act, establishing a bipartisan Civil Service Commission, competitive examinations, and appointment on merit. The Pendleton Act also gave the president
authority to extend by executive order the number of "classified" jobs—that is,
jobs subject to the merit system. The act applied initially only to about 14,000
of the more than 100,000 federal positions. But by the end of the 19th century
40 percent of federal jobs had moved into the classified category.

Civil service reform was in part a response to the growing complexity of
American life. As society grew more organized and problems more technical,
official duties were no longer so plain and simple that any person of intelligence
could perform them. In public service, as in other areas, the all-round man was
yielding ground to the expert, the amateur to the professional. The excesses
of the spoils system thus provoked the counter-ideal of scientific public administration, separate from politics and, as far as possible, insulated against it.

The cult of the expert, however, had its own excesses. The idea that
administration could be divorced from policy was an illusion. And in the realm
of policy, the expert, however much segregated from partisan politics, can

9

never attain perfect objectivity. He remains the prisoner of his own set of values. It is these values rather than technical expertise that determine fundamental judgments of public policy. To turn over such judgments to experts, moreover, would be to abandon democracy itself; for in a democracy final decisions must be made by the people and their elected representatives. "The business of the expert," the British political scientist Harold Laski rightly said, "is to be on tap and not on top."

Politics, however, were deeply ingrained in American folkways. This meant intermittent tension between the presidential government, elected every four years by the people, and the permanent government, which saw presidents come and go while it went on forever. Sometimes the permanent government knew better than its political masters; sometimes it opposed or sabotaged valuable new initiatives. In the end a strong president with effective cabinet secretaries could make the permanent government responsive to presidential purpose, but it was often an exasperating struggle.

The struggle within the executive branch was less important, however, than the growing impatience with bureaucracy in society as a whole. The 20th century saw a considerable expansion of the federal establishment. The Great Depression and the New Deal led the national government to take on a variety of new responsibilities. The New Deal extended the federal regulatory apparatus. By 1940, in a nation of 130 million people, the number of federal workers for the first time passed the 1 million mark. The Second World War brought federal civilian employment to 3.8 million in 1945. With peace, the federal establishment declined to around 2 million by 1950. Then growth resumed, reaching 2.8 million by the 1980s.

The New Deal years saw rising criticism of "big government" and "bureaucracy." Businessmen resented federal regulation. Conservatives worried about the impact of paternalistic government on individual self-reliance, on community responsibility, and on economic and personal freedom. The nation in effect renewed the old debate between Hamilton and Jefferson in the early republic, although with an ironic exchange of positions. For the Hamiltonian constituency, the "rich and well-born," once the advocate of affirmative government, now condemned government intervention, while the Jeffersonian constituency, the plain people, once the advocate of a weak central government and of states' rights, now favored government intervention.

In the 1980s, with the presidency of Ronald Reagan, the debate has burst out with unusual intensity. According to conservatives, government intervention abridges liberty, stifles enterprise, and is inefficient, wasteful, and

10

arbitrary. It disturbs the harmony of the self-adjusting market and creates worse troubles than it solves. Get government off our backs, according to the popular cliché, and our problems will solve themselves. When government is necessary, let it be at the local level, close to the people. Above all, stop the inexorable growth of the federal government.

In fact, for all the talk about the "swollen" and "bloated" bureaucracy, the federal establishment has not been growing as inexorably as many Americans seem to believe. In 1949, it consisted of 2.1 million people. Thirty years later, while the country had grown by 70 million, the federal force had grown only by 750,000. Federal workers were a smaller percentage of the population in 1985 than they were in 1955—or in 1940. The federal establishment, in short, has not kept pace with population growth. Moreover, national defense and the postal service account for 60 percent of federal employment.

Why then the widespread idea about the remorseless growth of government? It is partly because in the 1960s the national government assumed new and intrusive functions: affirmative action in civil rights, environmental protection, safety and health in the workplace, community organization, legal aid to the poor. Although this enlargement of the federal regulatory role was accompanied by marked growth in the size of government on all levels, the expansion has taken place primarily in state and local government. Whereas the federal force increased by only 27 percent in the 30 years after 1950, the state and local government force increased by an astonishing 212 percent.

Despite the statistics, the conviction flourishes in some minds that the national government is a steadily growing behemoth swallowing up the liberties of the people. The foes of Washington prefer local government, feeling it is closer to the people and therefore allegedly more responsive to popular needs. Obviously there is a great deal to be said for settling local questions locally. But local government is characteristically the government of the locally powerful. Historically, the way the locally powerless have won their human and constitutional rights has often been through appeal to the national government. The national government has vindicated racial justice against local bigotry, defended the Bill of Rights against local vigilantism, and protected natural resources against local greed. It has civilized industry and secured the rights of labor organizations. Had the states' rights creed prevailed, there would perhaps still be slavery in the United States.

The national authority, far from diminishing the individual, has given most Americans more personal dignity and liberty than ever before. The individual freedoms destroyed by the increase in national authority have been in the main the freedom to deny black Americans their rights as citizens; the freedom to put small children to work in mills and immigrants in sweatshops; the freedom to pay starvation wages, require barbarous working hours, and permit squalid working conditions; the freedom to deceive in the sale of goods and securities; the freedom to pollute the environment—all freedoms that, one supposes, a civilized nation can readily do without.

"Statements are made," said President John F. Kennedy in 1963, "labelling the Federal Government an outsider, an intruder, an adversary. . . . The United States Government is not a stranger or not an enemy. It is the people of fifty states joining in a national effort. . . . Only a great national effort by a great people working together can explore the mysteries of space, harvest the products at the bottom of the ocean, and mobilize the human, natural, and material resources of our lands."

So an old debate continues. However, Americans are of two minds. When pollsters ask large, spacious questions—Do you think government has become too involved in your lives? Do you think government should stop regulating business?—a sizable majority opposes big government. But when asked specific questions about the practical work of government—Do you favor social security? unemployment compensation? Medicare? health and safety standards in factories? environmental protection? government guarantee of jobs for everyone seeking employment? price and wage controls when inflation threatens?—a sizable majority approves of intervention.

In general, Americans do not want less government. What they want is more efficient government. They want government to do a better job. For a time in the 1970s, with Vietnam and Watergate, Americans lost confidence in the national government. In 1964, more than three-quarters of those polled had thought the national government could be trusted to do right most of the time. By 1980 only one-quarter was prepared to offer such trust. But by 1984 trust in the federal government to manage national affairs had climbed back to 45 percent.

Bureaucracy is a term of abuse. But it is impossible to run any large organization, whether public or private, without a bureaucracy's division of labor and hierarchy of authority. And we live in a world of large organizations. Without bureaucracy modern society would collapse. The problem is not to abolish bureaucracy, but to make it flexible, efficient, and capable of innovation.

Two hundred years after the drafting of the Constitution, Americans still regard government with a mixture of reliance and mistrust—a good combination. Mistrust is the best way to keep government reliable. Informed criticism

12

is the means of correcting governmental inefficiency, incompetence, and arbitrariness; that is, of best enabling government to play its essential role. For without government, we cannot attain the goals of the Founding Fathers. Without an understanding of government, we cannot have the informed criticism that makes government do the job right. It is the duty of every American citizen to know our government—which is what this series is all about.

Needy children are among the many groups that receive financial, medical, and other assistance from the Department of Health and Human Services (HHS)—the nation's "safety net." With the largest budget of any federal department, HHS runs several welfare programs, administers Social Security, distributes Medicaid and Medicare, and promotes public health.

ONE

The Unknown Department

Situation: You are 65 years old. After 40 years of backbreaking work as a farm laborer, you decide to retire. But you are not eligible for a pension program and your savings will keep you for only a few months. You have heard that the federal government provides financial support, called Social Security, to all retirees. Which federal department do you contact to obtain your Social Security benefits?

Situation: You are a poor woman with four children. Your husband has left home and refuses to pay child support. You find it impossible to hold a full-time job and take care of your children at the same time. What federal agency helps fund income-subsidy programs to assist poor, single-parent families like yours?

Situation: You are a Haitian refugee. You have fled your homeland to avoid political persecution. You have arrived in the United States without a job, with little money, with no knowledge of the language or customs and few contacts. What government organization will help you obtain education, job training, housing, and medical care?

Situation: You are an elderly woman suffering from chronic back problems that have forced you to be hospitalized repeatedly. The high cost of hospital care has depleted all of your savings. What department do you contact to sign up for federal medical insurance for the aged?

Situation: You are a scientist conducting important research on the causes of heart disease. You are on the verge of making a landmark discovery, but you have run out of funds. What government department do you contact to obtain a federal grant for medical research?

Most Americans could not answer these questions. The answer to all 5 is the Department of Health and Human Services (HHS), one of 14 federal departments with cabinet-level status (that is, their senior officials belong to the president's cabinet). In terms of budget, the HHS is the largest department in the federal government. Its budget constitutes approximately one-third of all federal outlays. It is staffed by 120,000 employees. Yet few Americans have heard of it.

HHS performs a multitude of functions. Stated in general terms, its role is to assist the needy and promote public health. To be more specific, it administers Social Security, which provides financial assistance for the elderly, the disabled, and survivors of deceased workers. It oversees two of the nation's four principal public assistance, or welfare, programs—Aid to Families with Dependent Children (AFDC), which provides income subsidies to poor one-parent families and two-parent families in which the primary breadwinner is unemployed; and Supplemental Security Income (SSI), which provides cash payments to aged, blind, and disabled people whose income is below a certain amount. (The other two are Food Stamps, which is handled by the Department of Agriculture, and Unemployment Insurance, which is managed by the Department of Labor.) And HHS supervises the government's two medical insurance programs—Medicare, an insurance program for the elderly, and Medicaid, an insurance program for the needy.

In the area of public health, the department helps control contagious diseases, works to strengthen the nation's hospitals, funds the training of health-care professionals, operates a vast network of medical research laboratories, serves as the largest source of funding for private medical research, protects consumers against unsafe food and drugs, and combats drug abuse. HHS also pays for and provides guidance to a wide array of state-operated social-service programs. These include programs that promote economic development on Indian reservations, help refugees settle in the United States, provide in-home care to the frail elderly, help single parents secure unpaid child support, and subsidize home-energy costs.

HHS's structure is quite complex. It includes five main divisions—the Social Security Administration, which administers Social Security; the Health Care Financing Administration, which administers Medicare and Medicaid; the Office of Human Development Services, which runs most of the federal

16

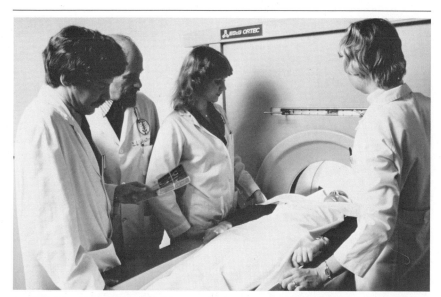

Public Health Service (PHS) doctors prepare to do a CAT scan, a computerized X ray, of a patient's brain. One of HHS's five operating divisions, the PHS oversees the nation's hospitals, conducts and funds medical research, fights the spread of infectious diseases, and protects consumers against unsafe food and drugs.

government's social-service programs; the Family Support Administration, which supervises the AFDC and social-service programs for families; and the Public Health Service, which promotes public well-being. Each division consists of several important bureaus and agencies, many of which are better known than HHS itself. For instance, the Public Health Service contains five major federal agencies—the Food and Drug Administration (FDA), the Centers for Disease Control (CDC), the National Institutes of Health (NIH), the Health Resources and Services Administration (HRSA), and the Alcohol, Drug Abuse, and Mental Health Administration (ADAMHA).

HHS serves the largest constituency of any federal department. Whereas the Department of Agriculture provides services to farmers, the Department of Labor assists American workers, and the Department of Commerce supports businesses, the HHS serves the blind, the elderly, the mentally ill, the retarded, children, families, American Indians, veterans, refugees, disadvantaged families, single-parent families—ultimately just about everyone in the United States. It is arguably the most important department in the federal government. Yet few people know about it. More Americans should.

17

President John Adams signs a 1798 law that directed the Treasury Department to provide medical insurance to merchant seamen and to set up a network of hospitals for sailors. The Public Health Service, HHS's oldest division, traces its origins to this law.

TWO

The Origins of HHS

The Department of Health and Human Services has existed in its present form only since 1979. But the federal government has been involved in promoting public health and providing social services almost since the nation was founded. During the 19th and early 20th centuries, this involvement was limited to providing medical care to merchant seamen, operating a small medical research laboratory, overseeing the national quarantine system, and running social-service programs for children, insane people, and freed slaves. But by the 1930s, federal funding for social programs had grown substantially and in 1939 a noncabinet-level agency, the Federal Security Administration, was established to coordinate all government activities in the areas of health, education, and welfare. In 1953, this agency was given cabinet-level status and its name was changed to the Department of Health, Education, and Welfare (HEW). In 1979, HEW's educational tasks were transferred to the new Department of Education and the remaining divisions of HEW were reorganized as the Department of Health and Human Services. Thus, although the history of the department itself is short, the story of its origins is not.

To a great extent, HHS is the product of several major social revolutions that took place between 1935 and 1968. The New Deal—President Franklin D. Roosevelt's slate of economic and social reforms aimed at combating the Great Depression—gave rise to the first federal programs for public assistance, unemployment insurance, old-age pensions, and disability payments. The health revolution, a marked rise in popular concern for health care after World War II, brought significant increases in federal funds for medical research and led to the enactment of Medicare and Medicaid legislation. The civil rights movement of the 1950s and 1960s convinced the government to expand vocational, educational, and other social programs for members of minority groups. And the consumer rights movement, launched by Ralph Nader during the 1960s, greatly expanded the government's role in protecting consumers from unsafe and unhealthy products. These revolutions resulted in the creation of billions of dollars' worth of social programs, most of which are today administered by the Department of Health and Human Services. Any history of HHS must examine these movements. But a full investigation of the department's origins must also consider the rich and lively early years of the few HHS bureaus and divisions that were established before the modern era.

HHS's Oldest Division

The oldest division of HHS is the Public Health Service, which traces its origins to a 1798 law that provided for the "care and relief of sick and disabled seamen." Signed by President John Adams, the law required the owners of American ships to withhold 20 cents a month from each crewman's wages and to forward the collected sum to a customs office in an American port. Customs officers, in turn, were to pass along the money to the secretary of the Treasury, who, under the guidance of the president, was to use the money to pay the hospital bills of injured or ill sailors. Federal authorities established the marine health program—despite the general practice in those days of leaving domestic policy to the states—because they considered healthy merchant marines to be crucial to the nation's economic success and self-defense. They realized that shipowners, states, and local governments were not interested in assuming this responsibility. The deduction of money from mariners' paychecks to pay for their medical bills constituted one of the first direct taxes levied by the federal government and was the nation's first medical insurance program. The idea was borrowed from Great Britain, which, using money deducted from seamen's wages, had established a hospital in Greenwich, England, to care for sailors wounded in the defeat of the Spanish Armada in 1588.

Under the 1798 law, the Treasury Department was authorized to use the money not only to pay sailors' medical bills, but also to construct new hospitals. A year after the law's passage, the first marine hospital was established in an

An 1827 view of the United States Marine Hospital in Chelsea, Massachusetts. By the early 19th century, the Treasury Department's network of marine hospitals, which was known as the Marine Hospital Service (MHS), stretched from Rhode Island to South Carolina.

abandoned barracks on Castle Island in Boston Harbor. Within a few years, an extensive network of marine hospitals had been set up in such ports as Norfolk, Virginia; Newport, Rhode Island; and Charleston, South Carolina. The network was known as the Marine Hospital Service (MHS), the predecessor of the Public Health Service.

In its first years, the MHS was plagued by administrative problems. No separate division existed within the Treasury Department to coordinate the activities of the individual hospitals. Members of the Treasury Department's general staff were too preoccupied with other duties to pay much attention to the MHS. Left to manage themselves, marine hospitals rarely cooperated with each other and adopted widely varying standards and procedures. Further problems arose because funds generated by withholding taxes from sailors' pay frequently fell short of the cost of providing medical services. Eventually, the MHS was forced to impose a four-month limit on the amount of time a patient

Upon arrival in the United States, immigrants are given physical examinations by uniformed members of the MHS's Commissioned Corps. The corps was established in 1889 as a pool from which the MHS's various branches could draw experienced medical personnel.

could stay in a marine hospital and to deny care to those with chronic or incurable ailments. MHS officials constantly had to appeal to Congress to allocate supplemental funds.

Recognizing that reforms were necessary, on June 29, 1870, Congress passed a bill that reorganized the MHS as an official national agency with a headquarters in Washington, D.C. Although it remained attached to the Treasury Department, the new agency was given its own administrative staff headed by an official called the supervising surgeon. The measure also raised the monthly medical tax on each sailor from 20 to 40 cents. John M. Woodward, the first supervising surgeon, immediately took steps to increase the agency's efficiency and to improve the quality of the care provided at its hospitals. He required all applicants for MHS jobs to pass a rigorous examination. He also mandated that surgeons at marine hospitals be appointed to the agency rather than to specific hospitals, to ensure that hiring would be done on the basis of merit rather than to appease local political groups.

Woodward launched the agency's first two publications—the annual report and a medical journal that remains in existence today under the title *Public Health Reports*.

Between 1870 and 1900, the MHS widened its focus significantly. Whereas in the past it had been concerned exclusively with the health of the merchant marine, it now took charge of several programs that involved the health of the general population. Under the First Quarantine Act, passed by Congress in 1878, it assumed responsibility for preventing the importation of infectious diseases by boat. It set up quarantine stations (posts where ships were detained in isolation) around the nation and gave each a fleet of inspection vessels. Agency inspectors intercepted ships before they reached port and examined cargoes and crews for traces of cholera, yellow fever, smallpox, bubonic plague, and other maladies. Ships found to be contaminated were sent back to sea or quarantined until the contagion subsided. In cooperation with the Bureau of Immigration, MHS doctors conducted physical examinations of immigrants, checking not only for disease but for other serious health problems that might disqualify them for admission to the country.

In 1887, the MHS took its first halting steps in medical research, setting up a one-room laboratory of hygiene at a marine hospital on Staten Island, New York. Directed by Dr. Joseph J. Kinyoun (a student of Robert Koch, the discoverer of the bacillus that causes tuberculosis) the lab concentrated initially

Dr. Joseph Kinyoun brought the MHS into the realm of medical research in 1887, setting up a laboratory of hygiene at a marine hospital on Staten Island, New York. Kinyoun's tiny, one-room lab was the forerunner of the National Institutes of Health.

23

on studying the environmental causes and biological makeup of acute diseases, and experimented with methods for treating and preventing them. Despite the laboratory's modest size, it managed to make notable contributions to the new science of *bacteriology* (the study of bacteria, microscopic organisms that can cause disease). It developed several types of disinfectant and designed a special fumigation apparatus. In 1891, Dr. Kinyoun's lab was renamed the Hygienic Laboratory and relocated to a more spacious facility in Washington, D.C. Eventually the lab would become the National Institutes of Health, which today has 12 divisions and spends about $6 billion a year on medical research.

To ensure that the MHS would have sufficient staff for its new activities, in 1889 Congress established a mobile force of physicians called the Commissioned Corps. The structure of the corps was adapted from the American military, with each doctor assigned a rank corresponding to a rank in the army and each subject to assignment anywhere in the United States. Corps members were used to staff quarantine stations and marine hospitals and to respond to outbreaks of disease, doctor shortages, and other health crises.

To help the MHS keep up with its expanded duties, in 1902 Congress passed a law that strengthened the agency's organization, clarified its chain of command, and established more definite guidelines for dividing its budget. The bill also gave the agency a greater role in coordinating the activities of local and state health authorities and changed its name to the Public Health and Marine Hospital Service (PHMHS) to reflect its broader concerns.

Early Social Programs

At the end of the Civil War the federal government had become involved for the first time in providing social services. At that time, 4 million recently freed slaves were having extreme difficulty starting a new life because of the lack of money and education and the ravaged condition of the Southern economy. Thousands of Southern whites uprooted by the war faced similar problems in finding new jobs and homes. To aid these groups—whom Southern states had neither the inclination nor the funds to assist—Congress and President Abraham Lincoln decided in March 1865 to set up the Freedmen's Bureau.

A branch of the War Department, the bureau was headed by a commissioner, General Oliver Otis Howard, and military officers. Officially titled the Bureau of Refugees, Freedmen, and Abandoned Lands, it was to provide food, shelter, job training and placement, and education. Bureau officials were directed to

A political poster from the Reconstruction era accuses the Freedmen's Bureau of encouraging laziness among blacks. Abraham Lincoln formed the bureau in 1865 to provide food, legal counsel, and job placement to freed slaves.

divide up lands abandoned by Southern farmers into 40-acre allotments and to help freedmen set up farms on the plots. They oversaw labor relations between freedmen and their employers, mediating labor disputes and drawing up contracts. And, in states where state courts refused to acknowledge the rights of blacks, the bureau set up temporary panels to hear cases involving freedmen. It is important to note, however, that bureau programs were limited to practical services and did not involve direct cash payments; not until 1935 would federal leaders accept the idea of giving financial support to the poor.

The era of the Freedmen's Bureau was short-lived. The bill establishing the bureau provided for it for only one year. In 1866, when Congress passed a law prolonging the bureau's operation, President Andrew Johnson, who had succeeded Lincoln in 1865, vetoed the legislation. He claimed that under the Constitution the federal government did not have the authority to set up social-service programs, only states did. Congress managed to override

Johnson's veto and to extend the bureau's operation until 1872. But by 1869, the bureau's responsibilities had largely been taken over by state governments, which were authorized to do so under the federal plan for Reconstruction. The hostility that was stirred up between the legislative and executive branches during the conflict over the constitutionality of the bureau made Congress reluctant for years thereafter to establish any new federal welfare agencies.

Lawmakers had no such qualms, however, about setting up social-service programs for the District of Columbia. No one could argue that welfare programs for the district would be better dealt with by the local government, because in this case, Congress was the local government. The first social legislation that Congress passed for the district was largely the product of lobbying by Dorothea Dix. An American social reformer born in 1802 in Hampden, Maine, Dix was distressed and angered by the poor treatment afforded mentally ill people in the United States. The usual course of action at the time was to place them in jail. During the 1840s and 1850s, Dix traveled more than 60,000 miles in the United States and Canada, pleading for a more humane approach to treatment for the mentally ill. She urged federal leaders to allot funds to each state for the purpose of establishing a mental hospital. In 1854, Congress passed a bill along these lines, but it was vetoed by President Franklin Pierce, who made the same charge of unconstitutionality later cited by President Johnson in 1866 in regard to the Freedmen's Bureau. Pierce could raise no such objections the following year when a measure was approved establishing a mental hospital in the District of Columbia. (Renamed St. Elizabeth's Hospital in 1916, it exists today as part of the National Institutes of Health.) Between 1857 and 1871, Congress created three additional social-service institutions in the district—the Columbia Institution for the Instruction of the Deaf and Dumb and the Blind, Howard University (a college for freedmen), and Freedmen's Hospital, which provided free health care to poor blacks.

The Progressive Era and the Expansion of Social Programs

Toward the end of the 19th century, the Industrial Revolution took hold in the United States, spawning considerable poverty in urban areas. Entrepreneurs set up large, impersonal factories in which the majority of work was performed by machines and unskilled laborers. Conditions in most plants were horrendous—hours were long, industrial accidents were common, child labor was widespread. Close to half of America's 38 million industrial workers lived in

Dorothea Dix, a Boston social reformer, spent most of her life crusading for fair treatment of the mentally ill. In 1855, she convinced Congress to set up the first government-financed mental hospital, which was built in the District of Columbia.

dilapidated tenements and overcrowded shantytowns, which often produced health crises and outbreaks of violence. By 1900, the richest 2 percent of Americans owned 60 percent of the nation's wealth.

Around that time, many members of the middle class—journalists, lawyers, social workers—initiated efforts to help the less privileged improve their lot. These reformers and the political groups they organized were known collectively as the Progressive movement. Progressive journalists and novelists attempted to expose the rest of the population to the miserable conditions in which the urban poor lived and worked. Social workers set up community centers and settlement houses to provide the disadvantaged with food, housing, education, and legal advice. Labor organizers assisted workers in forming unions to seek reduced hours, better working conditions, and higher wages. Out of a distrust of big government, however, most Progressives opposed having the government operate social programs, and most of those who did not favored placing such programs in the hands of the states. Even so, between 1900 and 1930 the Progressive movement gave rise to a modest increase in health and social programs at the federal level.

At the urging of Progressives such as Florence Kelley and Lillian Ward of the National Labor Committee, the federal government began to play a more active

Around the turn of the century, as millions of urban Americans were reduced to living in impoverished conditions such as those in this New York City tenement, the federal government made limited forays into the area of social welfare.

role in helping disadvantaged children. In 1908, President Theodore Roosevelt set up a White House conference on dependent children. And in 1912, Congress established a Children's Bureau to investigate "questions of infant mortality, the birth rate, orphanages, juvenile courts, desertion, dangerous occupations, accidents, diseases of children, employment, and legislation affecting children in the several states and territories."

Julia Clifford Lathrop, a social worker from Chicago, was named the first head of the Children's Bureau. Under her direction, the bureau devoted most of its resources to combating child labor—then defined as work by persons under 14 years of age. In 1916, it helped convince Congress to pass a law prohibiting the transport across state lines of products manufactured by factories that exploited children. The law remained in effect only until 1918, when the Supreme Court declared it unconstitutional. But in the meantime, the War Labor Policies Board, a temporary agency created to oversee labor relations during World War I, had begun requiring all companies that did business with the federal government to abandon the use of child labor. Pressure from Lathrop and her allies convinced President Woodrow Wilson to declare 1918 Children's Year, and to hold a conference on child-welfare standards in Washington, D.C., in May 1919. And in November 1921, Congress agreed, under the Sheppard-Towner Maternity and Infancy Hygiene Act, to provide federal funding to the states for maternal and infant health.

The Progressive era also brought expanded duties to the Public Health and Marine Hospital Service. Under the Biologics Control Act of 1902, the agency became responsible for monitoring the manufacture and sale of a class of drugs called *biologics* (biological products such as serums, toxins, and antitoxins that are used by doctors for medicinal purposes). Researchers at the Hygienic Laboratory were assigned to test each brand of biologic to make sure that it did not cause infections or other adverse reactions. The laboratory was also asked to establish standards of strength and potency for each biologic. The Biologics Control Act represented the first attempt by the federal government to regulate the sale of any kind of drug.

The PHMHS also enlarged its network of quarantine stations, setting up bases in Hawaii, Cuba, Puerto Rico, Panama, and the Philippine Islands. The service helped found two international organizations—the Pan-American Sanitary Bureau (1902), and the International Office of Public Health in Paris (1908). And it began conducting important field investigations. Two PHMHS scientists, Charles W. Stiles and Joseph Goldberger, made important contributions to science during their investigation of the parasite hookworm and the disease pellagra. PHMHS studies of health conditions in rural areas led many counties to increase their health and sanitation services. In Colorado and Missouri, a team of PHMHS researchers investigated *silicosis* (inflammation of the lungs caused by inhalation of silicate dust) among miners. And in Molokai, Hawaii, and Carville, Louisiana, the service set up research facilities to conduct studies of, and provide care for, victims of *leprosy* (a bacterial disease that causes the withering of skin and muscle tissue). A bill passed by Congress on August 14, 1912, authorized the service to launch an investigation of pollution in navigable rivers. The same law changed the agency's name to its present one—the Public Health Service.

Lagging Behind Europe

Until the Great Depression, public health and social services remained relatively low on the federal government's list of priorities. In 1929, Congress allocated only $19 million for the "promotion of public health"—about ⅓ of 1 percent of that year's federal budget. The federal government still had no programs in several areas of public health—the management of the nation's health-care delivery system, the distribution of hospital and medical services, and the provision of national insurance to cover hospital and medical care. Social services remained limited to the Children's Bureau and a few institutions in the District of Columbia. Furthermore, the government provided absolutely nothing in the way of financial assistance to disadvantaged groups. It offered no support for the aged, the disabled, or the ill and it accepted no responsibility for the poor. There was no insurance against unemployment and no system of public employment offices.

By contrast, during the late 19th and early 20th centuries most European nations had adopted the major components of the welfare state. In 1884, under Chancellor Otto von Bismarck, Germany became the first nation to provide

During the 1890s, poor people received free bean soup and bread at this wayfarers' lodge in Boston. Until the Great Depression, private charity groups, along with state and local governments, shouldered most of the burden for providing relief to the needy.

social insurance, allotting funds to help pregnant women pay medical costs. Six years later, it established a national system of old-age insurance and in 1927 adopted unemployment insurance. In 1897, workmen's compensation was set up in Great Britain, followed nine years later by old-age insurance, and three years after that by national health and unemployment insurance. By 1935, 22 European nations had some kind of social-security program.

The reluctance of the United States to follow Europe's lead in offering protection against the hazards of the industrial age and providing assistance to the poor could be traced in large part to the impact of the frontier on the nation's development. During the 19th century, the abundance of opportunities on the frontier made welfare programs seem unnecessary to most Americans. It was thought that people who lost their jobs or for some other reason had difficulty making ends meet could always migrate westward, where acres of productive farmland were available for anyone with a willingness to work hard. Those who remained impoverished in the midst of such plenty, Americans reasoned, had only themselves to blame.

By the turn of the century, the frontier had very nearly disappeared. Still, American farmers—their view distorted by a fierce self-reliance acquired during the process of settling the heartland—continued to believe that jobs were available for everyone who was sufficiently persistent. And by and large this point of view continued to dominate the national atmosphere. Congressmen from rural areas, who shared the individualistic credo of their constituents, exerted a disproportionate influence on key congressional committees. Assisted by the lobbying efforts of wealthy industrialists, these conservative congressmen effectively blocked all attempts to establish social insurance at the federal level. If social-welfare programs had been established at the federal level they probably would have been invalidated by the Supreme Court as unconstitutional intrusions into an area reserved for the states. In case after case, the justices had ruled that all major domestic tasks belonged to the states—on the basis of a clause in the Tenth Amendment to the Constitution, which states, "The powers not delegated to the United States . . . are reserved to the states respectively, or to the people."

Ultimately, the job of providing relief to the needy largely fell to private charity groups and state and local governments. In the 1920s, 30 states established some form of old-age pension. An even greater number set up a mother's pension—a program in which widows with children received financial support. It would take a major crisis, the Great Depression, to convince American leaders to establish welfare programs at the national level.

Worried investors crowd the pavement on Wall Street in October 1929 after stock market values took a precipitous drop. The stock market crash triggered the worst economic depression in American history.

THREE

The Rise of the Welfare State

Herbert Hoover took office as president of the United States in January 1929, declaring in his inaugural address that he had "no fears for the future of our country. It is bright with hope." Most Americans shared his optimism, having lived through a period of unrivaled economic prosperity. On Wall Street, investors in the stock market, believing the boom would never end, bought every share of stock they could get their hands on, driving up the value of issues far beyond their actual worth. Then came the crash.

In October 1929, investors panicked and sold off millions of shares in a matter of days, causing the market to drop precipitously. In the process, thousands of *speculators* (people who buy or sell stocks hoping to make a profit from fluctuations in the market) lost everything they owned. At first, it appeared that these investors would be the only victims. But as it turned out, the Wall Street crash marked the beginning of the worst economic depression in U.S. history.

The Great Depression

Even before the panic, the economy had shown signs of weakness, in spite of Hoover's insistence that "the fundamental business of the country is on a sound and prosperous basis." Beginning as early as June 1929, industrial production had begun to fall and unemployment to rise, diminishing the power of consumers to purchase goods. At the same time, industrial investment also dropped. When the crash occurred, it turned these cracks in the economic foundation into major chasms. By wiping out savings and destroying confidence in the economy, the crash slowed consumer spending to a trickle. As inventories piled up, companies instituted massive layoffs. A debilitating cycle developed in which higher unemployment led to further shortages in purchasing power, which led to additional rounds of layoffs—and so on. Between 1930 and 1932, the ranks of the unemployed grew from 4 million to 11 million. Those who managed to hold onto their job saw their wages reduced drastically. Between 1929 and 1933, labor income dropped from $53 billion to $31.5 billion. As time went on, an increasing number of companies were forced to declare bankruptcy. With more and more real estate and commercial loans in default, many banks failed.

For millions of lower- and middle-class Americans, the pattern was the same: After losing their job, their income dwindled, they lost their savings, they lost their insurance, and unable to keep up with their mortgages, they lost their homes. Without money, they hawked their furniture, their keepsakes, their clothes, and finally, they were forced to seek aid from soup kitchens and breadlines. Many took up residence in shacks built of empty packing boxes in temporary shantytowns that sprung up on the outskirts of several cities. Others took to the open road, hitchhiking and sneaking onto trains, under the misconception that conditions were different in other parts of the country. A nation "bright with hope" had been reduced to a nation grim with despair.

Hoover, an outspoken advocate of free enterprise, refused to take drastic action to remedy the nation's ills. He did urge companies not to cut wages and supported a shorter workday as a way of spreading available work among as many people as possible. And in 1932, he endorsed the establishment of a federal agency called the Reconstruction Finance Corporation (RFC) to subsidize construction and investment. But, in the words of one historian, these measures were like "applying band-aids to third-degree body burns."

Creating Social Security

In the 1932 presidential election, voters expressed their disapproval of Hoover's policies, rejecting him in favor of Democratic candidate Franklin D. Roosevelt, the former governor of New York. In his inaugural address, Roosevelt pledged immediate and far-reaching action to ease the effects of the

*Unemployed men gather in front of a shack in New York City in 1938.
Widespread unemployment and poverty during the Great Depression
led an increasing number of Americans to support federal involvement in social welfare.*

depression, reassuring the American people with the memorable words, "The
only thing we have to fear is fear itself." With the American people behind him
and an overwhelming Democratic majority in Congress, Roosevelt was able to
bring about an extraordinary program of emergency relief and work measures
during his first 100 days in office.

Roosevelt convinced lawmakers to supply federal cash to bail out state and
local welfare agencies. He also set up a host of public-works projects to provide
jobs for the unemployed. The first was the Civilian Conservation Corps (CCC),
which provided unemployed and underprivileged men between the ages of 18
and 25 with vocational training in the conservation of natural resources. Other
public works projects included the Civil Works Administration (CWA), which
during the harsh winter of 1933–34 gave 4 million people temporary jobs
building roads and schoolhouses; the National Youth Administration (NYA),

Two employees of the Civilian Conservation Corps (CCC) work on an agricultural project in 1935. One of many public works agencies established by President Franklin D. Roosevelt to combat the depression, the CCC provided jobs for men aged 18 to 25.

which provided part-time jobs to underprivileged college and high school students and full-time jobs to dropouts; and the Public Works Administration (PWA), which provided work on major construction projects such as schools, hospitals, public housing, and dams.

These programs served as the foundation of the New Deal. But in Roosevelt's view, they were only stopgap measures. He believed that the federal government should create a permanent structure to ensure the economic security of workers in good times and bad. And he was not the only one who held this view. Having seen millions of respectable, hardworking, middle-class people lose their jobs through no fault of their own, many Americans had abandoned the belief that the poor were to blame for their condition and relinquished their opposition to federal involvement in welfare programs. A number of political groups around the nation issued plans for government assistance to the poor. Under the leadership of Dr. Francis E. Townsend of California, thousands of aged Americans (a group hit particularly hard by the depression) demanded that Washington provide pensions of $200 a month to all persons over the age of 65. The writer Upton Sinclair vied for the governorship of California on a platform that promised to "End Poverty." Huey Long, a Democratic senator from Louisiana, put forth the Share The Wealth plan—under which funds for the poor would be raised by confiscating the property of the rich. Ultimately, Roosevelt realized that failure to enact a comprehensive social-insurance system might jeopardize his chances in the 1936 presidential election.

In the summer of 1934 he created a temporary panel of experts to draw up a long-range social program. Called the Committee on Economic Security, it was chaired by Frances Perkins, the secretary of labor and the first woman cabinet member, and was assisted by a Technical Board and a 23-member Advisory Council. For guidance, members studied the social programs of several European countries and consulted American social workers and scholars. Their task was not an easy one; among other difficult questions, they had to address the possibility that a direct federal welfare program might be unconstitutional. Nevertheless, like most New Deal teams, they accomplished their task with remarkable speed, coming up with a proposal by December 1934.

Their plan called for three basic programs. The first was an old-age insurance program, under which all retired people over the age of 65 were to receive regular income subsidies. It was to be administered by the federal government and funded by a payroll tax shared by management and workers. The second program was unemployment compensation, which was to be operated by the states but funded by a federal payroll tax on employers, and guided by benefit minimums established by federal law. The third was a program of public assistance for the destitute aged and families with dependent children, to be financed by the federal government and administered by the states. The first two programs were called social insurance because they promised to insure workers against the hazards of old age and unemployment and because they would be operated like insurance plans—with premiums paid by employers and employees supporting a central fund out of which benefit payments would be made. The third was known as public assistance because it was to be financed directly by the federal government and—unlike the insurance program, whose recipients could be at any income level—it would supply aid only to the needy (as determined by so-called means tests).

Perkins and her fellow committee members also gave thought to proposing national medical insurance, but decided the nation was not yet ready for it. Instead, they recommended moderate increases in the federal role in public health. They suggested that federal monies be made available to the states to fund maternal and child health services, to pay for crippled children's services, and to help expand state and local health departments.

The programs recommended by the committee were known collectively as Social Security, although in later years many people would come to associate the term only with the old-age pension program. In developing Social Security, the committee took pains to tailor the European idea of social insurance to fit conditions in the United States. For instance, they provided for extensive involvement by the states as a way of pacifying those who objected, on constitutional grounds, to direct federal welfare programs. The plan also rejected the notion—popular in Europe—that welfare programs should be used to reapportion national income to give each person his or her fair share. Instead, it accommodated the American preference for giving public support only to those who could not help themselves.

President Roosevelt signs the Social Security Act on August 15, 1935. The act went beyond temporary relief programs, setting up a permanent structure to safeguard workers against the hazards of unemployment and old age.

In 1937, in a decision written by Justice Benjamin H. Cardozo, the Supreme Court upheld the constitutionality of the Social Security Act and gave Congress broad powers to institute new social programs.

Roosevelt approved the committee's recommendations and submitted the Social Security Act to Congress in January 1935. It encountered severe opposition from several groups, including the National Association of Manufacturers, the United States Chamber of Commerce, and most Republican lawmakers. In some quarters, it was described disparagingly as *socialistic* (reminiscent of states in which the government controls the means of production and the distribution of goods). But ultimately, the Democratic majority pushed the bill through in much the same form as had been proposed by the Perkins committee. The only significant change was that blind people were added to the list of groups who would receive public assistance. On August 15, 1935, Roosevelt signed the bill, officially enacting the most important piece of social legislation ever passed. (By the 1980s, Social Security would account for more than 20 percent of the federal budget.) To administer the new programs, Congress established an independent three-member Social Security Board, to be appointed by the president.

Almost as soon as the new agency opened its doors, old-age insurance and unemployment compensation were disputed in court as violations of the Tenth Amendment to the Constitution. In 1937, the Supreme Court agreed to rule on

A Social Security Board (SSB) advertisement urges people to take advantage of the old-age insurance program, under which retired workers 65 and older received income supplements. Using such ads, the SSB quickly eliminated initial opposition to the program.

the constitutionality of the programs. Dominated at the time by conservative justices, the panel seemed likely to outlaw the Social Security Act. But instead, in a decision written by Associate Justice Benjamin N. Cardozo, the Court not only upheld the law but also gave Congress the green light to pass any further legislation it thought necessary to "promote the general welfare." It was a landmark event in the history of the welfare state. In subsequent years, freed from doubt about its constitutional authority to establish social policy, Congress drastically stepped up its involvement in health, education, and welfare. Between 1937 and 1972, federal expenditures in these areas rose from $2.5 billion to $84 billion.

The Social Security Board

The Cardozo decision helped disarm many of Social Security's critics. Public relations efforts by the Social Security Board further eliminated opposition to federal social insurance. In particular, the board was successful in changing the old-age insurance program's reputation from that of "despised dole" to a "popular government program," in the words of historian Rufus E. Miles, Jr., by stressing the contributory nature of the program. During its first years, the board also performed with distinction in several other areas: recruiting talented employees, setting up cost-effective procedures for administering social insurance, and providing old-age pensions in a way that satisfied the majority of recipients.

The board's success had much to do with the effective leadership of Arthur Altmeyer, who served as an influential member from 1935 to 1946. Altmeyer was the perfect blend of the bureaucrat and the politician. On the one hand, he was unpretentious and nonpartisan, a skillful manager with a broad knowledge

Arthur Altmeyer testifies before the House Ways and Means Committee. Altmeyer served on the Social Security Board from 1935 to 1946 and as Social Security commissioner from 1946 to 1953.

of social policy and an eye for detail. On the other hand, he was a master of the kind of political maneuvering that was necessary to influence the president and to get bills passed.

Throughout Altmeyer's tenure, he sought to expand Social Security, regarding it as an effective but incomplete system. In 1939, he and his colleagues convinced Congress to pass an amendment to the Social Security Act that established a benefit program for widows and minor children of workers. Called survivor's insurance, it was, like old-age insurance, wholly administered by the federal government and financed by payroll taxes on employers and employees. Also contained in the 1939 bill was an article that required states involved in administering Social Security programs to hire employees for those programs on the basis of merit. Prior to that time, most state workers received jobs as a reward for their political loyalty. Few states had regular procedures for raises, promotions, and retirement. But in response to the merit-system provisions in the new bill, states established highly comprehensive personnel systems that continue to be in use today.

The Brownlow Committee

The Social Security Board was only one of many new executive agencies that emerged from the Roosevelt administration's efforts to defeat the Great Depression. Most of these new organizations were asked to report directly to the president. As time went on, however, it became clear that Roosevelt could not supervise all of them. Meanwhile, federal leaders realized that several agencies created during previous administrations had been inappropriately assigned to larger departments. (The Public Health Service's assignment to the Department of the Treasury was a prime example.)

With these concerns in mind, Roosevelt set up a committee to develop a plan for reorganizing the federal bureaucracy. Consisting of three career government workers, Louis Brownlow, Luther Gutlick, and Charles Merriam, it was known as the President's Committee on Administrative Management, or the Brownlow Committee. In its initial report, completed in 1937, the committee recommended the establishment of a new government mechanism whereby reorganization proposals submitted by the president to Congress would automatically become law unless acted upon within 60 days. Always receptive to the idea of expanding executive power, Roosevelt welcomed the proposal. Taking advantage of the Democratic congressional majority, he convinced lawmakers to establish such a mechanism in an April 1939 bill.

Then, he asked the committee to prepare a second report outlining specific proposals for using the president's new powers to revamp the government. When other federal officials got wind of the committee's assignment, they hounded its members, pleading their cases for and against reorganization. To escape the constant pressure, Brownlow chose to go into hiding until the plan was complete. In the end, three major actions were urged:

- Removing the Bureau of the Budget from the Department of the Treasury and making it the foundation of a new Executive Office of the President.
- Merging most of the New Deal public-works programs into a body called the Federal Works Agency.
- Establishing a Federal Security Agency (FSA) in order to consolidate all agencies dealing with health, education, and welfare.

Committee members had initially proposed to call the latter institution the Department of Social Welfare instead of the FSA, but they were discouraged from doing so by Vice-president John Nance Garner, who insisted that, to most Americans, the term *welfare* suggested wasteful government handouts. The word *security*—which at the time referred to economic security rather than defense—was thought to be preferable because of its association with Social Security, which had become a popular program. The Brownlow Committee had also wanted to make the FSA a cabinet-level department but, under the April 1939 law, the president could use his new powers to create only lower-level agencies.

Roosevelt was pleased with the plan and submitted it to Congress. After Congress's 60-day deadline had expired, the bill became law and the Federal Security Agency, the first of HHS's predecessors, came into being. As Louis Brownlow wrote in his memoirs, *A Passion for Anonymity*, the new agency was "in everything but words a major department." The FSA differed from cabinet-level bodies, according to Brownlow, only in that its head was called an administrator instead of a secretary and received a $9,000 salary instead of the $10,000 a cabinet officer was given. Its primary components were the Social Security Board, the Public Health Service, which was transferred from the Department of the Treasury, and the Office of Education, which was transferred from the Department of the Interior. (The Office of Education had been established in 1867 to conduct educational research. The office gathered information on the management, organization, and teaching methods of the nation's schools and provided it to state governments, which retained authority for actually running the schools.)

Also incorporated into the FSA were the Government Printing House for the Blind, two public-works agencies—the National Youth Administration and the Civilian Conservation Corps—and the U.S. Employment Service, which ran job training and placement programs and had previously belonged to the Department of Labor. In 1940, the FSA took over the Department of the Interior's responsibility for managing four District of Columbia social-service institutions established by Congress during the 1800s—St. Elizabeth's Hospital, Freedmen's Hospital, the Columbia Institution for the Deaf (Gallaudet College), and Howard University. In the same year, the Food and Drug Administration was transferred to the FSA from the Department of Agriculture. The FDA had been created in 1927 to enforce the 1906 Pure Food and Drug Act, which set standards for the purity and safety of food and drugs. The act had previously been administered by the Bureau of Chemistry.

In 1940 the Federal Security Administration (FSA) took over management of Howard University (shown here) in Washington, D.C., from the Department of the Interior.

44

Former Indiana governor Paul V. Mc-Nutt and his wife pose for news photographers. McNutt served as head of the FSA during World War II, adjusting the agency's activities to the new demands of wartime.

The Federal Security Administration (1939–1953)

During its 14-year history, the FSA had 3 administrators: Paul V. McNutt (1939–45), who had previously served as governor of Indiana; Watson B. Miller (1945–47), an official with the American Legion; and Oscar R. Ewing (1947–53), a corporate lawyer and former vice-chairman of the Democratic party. Soon after McNutt took office, World War II broke out, resulting in significant changes for the country and for the FSA. The expansion of industry to produce war supplies created millions of new jobs and virtually eliminated the need for public works agencies. Consequently, the FSA's two public works agencies, the Civilian Conservation Corps and the National Youth Administration, were quickly disbanded.

At the same time, the FSA, like most federal agencies, was given special wartime tasks. The Public Health Service carried out emergency health and sanitary measures and added a temporary Office of Malaria Control to help military units avoid and combat the disease in war areas. FSA divisions that could be used to mobilize workers for wartime industry gained prominence. The U.S. Employment Service placed millions of workers in new jobs during the war. The Education Office offered short-term courses to train newcomers to heavy industry, including many women. With labor shortages widespread and industrial accidents on the rise, the Education Office's Vocational Rehabilitation Program, which helped disabled workers reenter the workplace, was expanded considerably. In 1943, the program was removed from the Education Office and made into a new FSA agency called the Office of Vocational Rehabilitation. Among other duties, it was put in charge of administering grants to the states for vocational rehabilitation.

To coordinate the activities of the many federal agencies involved in mobilizing the work force, the War Manpower Commission was established and McNutt was named chairman. The FSA administrator retained his regular post but his new duties took up most of his time and, as a result, many of the FSA's smaller divisions—such as Howard University and the Columbia Institution for the Deaf—received little guidance from him.

As hundreds of new factories and military bases sprung up across the country, new social problems developed. For example, the movement of large segments of the population to areas where industry was concentrated stretched local health and welfare services to the limit. To cope with such problems, a new FSA agency, the Office of Defense, Health, and Welfare Services, was formed in 1941. It was assigned to help with the construction of new hospitals and schools in communities adjacent to military bases and munitions plants; to make sure that health-care professionals were distributed around the country in accordance with population; and to combat the alarming rise of venereal disease that had accompanied massive population shifts. After the war ended, the FSA resumed normal operations. The War Manpower Commission, the Office of Defense, Health, and Welfare Services, and most other special wartime agencies and programs were dismantled. One exception was the Office of Vocational Rehabilitation's grants program, which went on to become one of the most effective programs of the Department of Health, Education, and Welfare. In 1946, the FSA was again revamped, under an executive order issued by President Harry S. Truman.

Reorganization Plan Number 2 of 1946 shifted the Children's Bureau from the Department of Labor to the FSA, except for programs that involved child labor. The move stirred up considerable ill will among the women who ran the bureau. Not only was their bureau being split down the middle, it was being removed from a department that had easy access to the president and was being put under the command of an official who did not even belong to the cabinet. The reorganization plan also disbanded the Social Security Board's three-man management team and redelegated its authority to the Federal Security administrator. The move reflected the belief popular among government bureaucrats that heads of agencies, in order to perform their jobs to the fullest, had to be given direct control of all of their subdivisions. Under the new arrangement, the Social Security Board was renamed the Social Security Administration.

The postwar period saw the Public Health Service expand significantly. By this time, the American people had come to expect better service from hospitals and doctors in light of rapid advances in medical research, technology, and care. They also had become more interested in and knowledgeable about good health and had come to accept the idea of vigorous federal action to guarantee adequate health care. In response to this transformation in values,

A United States Employment Service office. Because of the expansion of industry during World War II, the Employment Service was able to place millions of unemployed people in new jobs.

Senator John L. McClellan (left), chairman of the Senate Expenditures Committee, and former president Herbert Hoover discuss government reorganization at a Hoover Commission meeting. Congress rejected the commission's 1949 proposal to reorganize the FSA.

which is often referred to as the health revolution, in 1944 Congress began to enact a spate of legislation that, over the years, markedly increased federal funds for private medical research, expanded the government's own research programs, stepped up federal allotments to state health departments, and transformed the Public Health Service into one of the biggest agencies outside the cabinet.

The first such bill, the Public Health Service Act of 1944, enlarged the agency's role in medical research and authorized it to grant fellowships to aspiring doctors in training programs. The bill also reorganized the service to enable it to deal with its increased responsibilities. It was divided into four main units: the Office of the Surgeon General, the Bureau of Medical Services, the Bureau of State Services, and the National Institute of Health (as the Hygienic Laboratory had been renamed in 1930).

In 1946, the Public Health Service became involved for the first time in efforts to improve and enlarge the nation's health-care delivery system. During the 1930s and early 1940s, as a result of economic depression and wartime

48

shortages of building materials, the construction of new hospitals had not kept pace with population increases. At the same time, many existing facilities had fallen into disrepair or had become obsolete. Under the 1946 Hill-Burton Act, the PHS began providing financial and technical assistance for the construction of new hospitals and the modernization of old ones. Also in 1946, the PHS assumed three other important tasks. It took over from the Bureau of the Census responsibility for producing national vital statistics. Under the National Mental Health Act, it established a national advisory council on mental health and made grants available for the training of mental-health professionals, research on mental-health problems, and operation of community health facilities. And it transformed the temporary Office of Malaria Control into the permanent Communicable Disease Center, which was assigned the development of techniques for controlling the spread of infectious diseases.

In 1948, the federal government's participation in medical research grew enormously as the National Institute of Health created a host of subdivisions—the National Heart Institute, the National Institute of Dental Research, the National Microbiological Institute, and the Experimental Biology and Medicine Institute. To reflect these additions, the NIH's name was changed to the plural designation National Institutes of Health.

During the late 1940s, President Truman urged lawmakers to give the FSA status as a cabinet-level department. The Hoover Commission, a temporary panel set up under the leadership of former president Herbert Hoover to examine ways to reorganize the government, endorsed the proposal. But when a bill to reorganize the FSA came before Congress in 1949, it was rejected— as a result of lobbying efforts by the American Medical Association (AMA), whose members feared that any expansion of federal powers in the area of health would be tantamount to establishing *socialized medicine* (assumption of all medical care and costs by the government). Also opposed to the measure were officials of some of the FSA subdivisions, who instead wanted independence for their agencies. In 1949, Congress did agree to one change in FSA operations—the transfer of the unemployment compensation program from the Social Security Administration to the Department of Labor. But, ironically, it would not be until Congress was controlled by Republicans—who had traditionally argued against the expansion of social programs—that the FSA would attain departmental status.

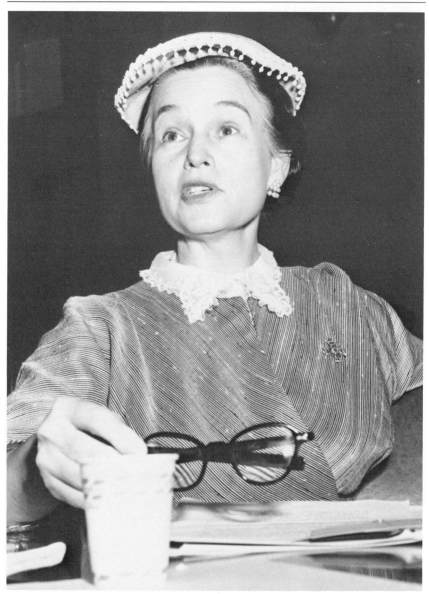

In 1953, President Dwight D. Eisenhower gave the FSA cabinet-level status and renamed it the Department of Health, Education, and Welfare (HEW). Oveta Culp Hobby (shown here) was appointed as the new department's first secretary, becoming only the second woman in American history to serve in a president's cabinet.

FOUR

As HEW: Expansion and Controversy

When he took office as president in 1953, Dwight D. Eisenhower believed he needed to initiate some kind of immediate and dramatic action to capture the attention of the country. He decided that the boldest move possible would be to create a cabinet-level welfare department along the lines proposed by Truman. He appointed Oveta Culp Hobby to head the Federal Security Administration and directed her to develop plans for such a department.

Hobby had enjoyed an interesting career. During World War II she had served as commander of the Women's Army Corps and had become acquainted with Eisenhower, who was then in charge of the European theater of operations. After the war, she had served as editor and publisher of the Houston *Post*. She had been active in the Democratic party ever since her appointment, at the age of 21, as *parliamentarian* (expert on legislative rules) of the Texas legislature. In spite of her political affiliations, she had campaigned vigorously for Eisenhower, a Republican, in the 1952 presidential election.

By the time Hobby took office, the president had gained the power to create cabinet-level departments by executive order, subject to congressional veto. Hobby's task was essentially to draft such an order—with the assistance of officials from the Executive Office of the President and FSA staff. From the outset she and her aides realized that the plan should be kept simple to minimize congressional and popular resistance. They agreed to propose three actions: changing the FSA's name, making its director a member of the cabinet, and giving its director power to appoint an under secretary, three assistant secretaries, and a general counsel.

Translating these basic proposals into a formal plan proved harder than they had expected. They had particular difficulty settling on an appropriate name for the new department. In the interest of brevity, some favored the name Department of Welfare, but the majority disapproved of the idea, believing that it would offend many of the ardently antiwelfare members of the Republican party. Another faction proposed the title Department of the General Welfare— a phrase from the preamble to the U.S. Constitution—but this was rejected as being "too presumptuous for the most junior of the departments," in the words of historian Rufus E. Miles, Jr. A third suggestion, Department of Human Resources, was discarded because it seemed to suggest that people were simply resources to be used by the government, thus recalling the detached mentality of many totalitarian states. A fourth idea, Department of Health, Education, and Social Security, fell by the wayside after officials discovered that its acronym was HESS, the last name of the man who had served as Adolf Hitler's second-in-command in Nazi Germany. In the end, the title Department of Health, Education, and Welfare was deemed the most acceptable, in spite of its length and lack of elegance.

The Second Woman in the Cabinet

In 1953 Hobby's plan was submitted to Congress, where it was approved with little opposition. (It passed 291 to 86 in the House and 99 to 1 in the Senate.) On April 11, 1953, Hobby was sworn in as the first secretary of health, education, and welfare, becoming only the second woman in American history to belong to a president's cabinet. The new department inherited all of the divisions and programs of the FSA—including the Office of Education, the Social Security Administration, the Public Health Service, the Food and Drug Administration, and the National Institutes of Health. For a new department, it was quite large. It was served by more than 34,000 employees and had an

An inspector for the Food and Drug Administration (FDA), one of HEW's original divisions, tests samples of vitamin B1. During her two-year tenure, Secretary Hobby significantly enlarged the FDA's staff and increased its budget.

annual budget of $5.4 billion ($3.4 billion of which was spent on Social Security benefits). At the time, however, federal officials had no conception of how many new responsibilities it would inherit over the following 26 years.

During its first days, the Department of Health, Education, and Welfare attracted a great deal of attention from the press and public. In part the interest in HEW reflected a tendency among the news media to take more interest in cabinet-level departments than in lower-level agencies. It also reflected a fascination with the secretary herself. Newspapers gave extensive coverage both to Hobby's official actions and to her social engagements.

HEW's honeymoon with the public and press was soon shattered, however, by attacks on Social Security. A number of congressmen and interest groups faulted the system for being too strict in its eligibility requirements. At the time, several major groups were excluded from coverage—farmers, domestic servants, employees of nonprofit organizations, and the self-employed. Some federal leaders went so far as to propose eliminating the contributory feature of the system to make it a simple pension program. But Hobby moved quickly to halt the rising tide of opposition to Social Security, establishing a committee of outside consultants to evaluate social-insurance programs. The committee found the system to be effective as far as it went but recommended that coverage be extended to farm and domestic workers. On September 1, 1954, Congress made these proposals law, thereby opening up Social Security to 10 million new beneficiaries. The new Social Security bill was passed with a huge bipartisan majority in both houses of Congress and restored most Americans' approval of the social-insurance system.

In spite of her early success, as time went on Hobby became the target of increasing criticism from Congress, much of which was unjustified. Members of the House of Representatives derided her for enlarging her own staff through the use of funds meant for HEW programs. In retrospect, her action seems perfectly warranted—the executive order establishing HEW had given her a much smaller office than any of the other cabinet-level departments. Many Democratic congressmen also lambasted her for proceeding too slowly in establishing new health and welfare programs. They were particularly dismayed by her opposition to federal aid for education. Some lawmakers referred to her as the "Secretary of Not Too Much Health, Education, and Welfare."

But to be fair to the secretary, her seeming resistance to new social programs was in large part dictated by orders from her boss. And, in truth, she was responsible for winning the passage of several bills. During her tenure, the Vocational Rehabilitation Program was enlarged by 400 percent. She increased funds for the construction of chronic disease hospitals, nursing homes, rehabilitation centers, and diagnostic and treatment centers. And with the help of Assistant Secretary Bradshaw Mintener, she strengthened the FDA, which had gone for many years without any increase in staff levels, despite taking on several new duties. In 1955, she appointed a Citizens Committee on Food and Drugs to assess the FDA's effectiveness. The committee's final report, which urged significant expansion of the FDA, helped counteract claims by congressmen that the agency placed an undue burden on industry. It also resulted in a fourfold increase in the FDA's size over the following 10 years.

During Hobby's last months in office, her department was thrust into the national spotlight when it was assigned to distribute a polio vaccine that had just been discovered by Dr. Jonas Salk. Earlier in the century, there had been several severe outbreaks of *polio* (an acute infectious disease, found mostly in children, that attacks the spinal cord causing high fever and often paralysis), so millions of parents across the country were anxious to obtain the drug. The problem was that there was not enough of it to go around. Consequently, HEW had to develop a priority system for administering it—an extremely delicate task. The department had to contend with wealthy parents who thought they should be entitled to early access to the vaccine. Many criticized HEW for taking too long to release the vaccine, and one group, the Americans for Democratic Action, called for Hobby's ouster. Eventually, the pressure of the emergency task overwhelmed Hobby and, in the summer of 1955, she resigned.

Funds for Education and Medical Research

Hobby was replaced by Under Secretary of the Treasury Marion B. Folsom. As an executive of the Eastman Kodak Company earlier in the decade, Folsom had played a major role in convincing big business to accept the principle of social insurance. During his three-year term as secretary of HEW, Folsom devoted much of his time to lobbying for increased federal aid for education. For years President Eisenhower had been opposed to the idea. But Folsom arranged a dramatic presentation for the president in which he painted a grim portrait of the nation's educational system: As a result of the postwar baby boom, there were 2 million more students than the system could accommodate. This put an enormous burden on taxpayers—schools operated primarily with funds generated by state property taxes. The nation needed more than 80,000 new classrooms but the states were unable to pay for them.

After hearing these distressing statistics, the president gave Folsom the go-ahead to develop a plan for increased federal involvement in education. While Folsom was doing so, the Soviet Union launched *Sputnik*, the first artificial satellite, in September 1957. The launching shocked Americans, who had always considered the nation's technology and science to be far superior to

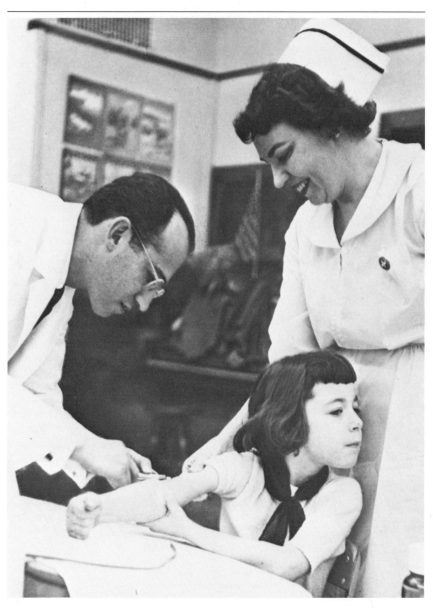

Dr. Jonas Salk, who developed an effective vaccine against polio in 1954, administers it to a young patient. In 1955, HEW was put in charge of distributing the then-scarce vaccine. Criticism of the department's handling of the task prompted Secretary Hobby to resign from office.

those of the other superpower. Many were convinced that drastic changes were needed in the American educational system. With this ground swell of support for increased attention to education, in 1958 Folsom was able to push through Congress the National Defense Education Act, which allotted $900 million in federal aid for education in mathematics, science, and foreign languages.

Folsom also encouraged Eisenhower to endorse increased spending for medical research. Each year, Eisenhower had called for modest boosts in allocations for the National Institutes of Health and each year Congress had embarrassed him by allocating millions more than was requested. In 1957, Folsom formed a high-level HEW advisory committee on biomedical research that helped convince Eisenhower to increase his research request. But Congress rejected even this proposal and poured still more money into the NIH's budget—as it would do for several years thereafter.

During Folsom's time in office, Social Security was expanded to include social insurance for people who were unable to work for more than a year because of illness or injury. His tenure also saw an increase in federal aid for the construction of medical centers. In 1955, responsibility for the health care of American Indians and Alaska natives was transferred from the Department of the Interior to the Public Health Service. And, in 1957, the HEW was assigned to administer the Asian flu vaccine.

Cranberries and Illegitimate Children

Because of ill health, Folsom had to resign from office in 1958. He was succeeded by Dr. Arthur S. Flemming, the president of Ohio University. His two and a half years as secretary were characterized primarily by the quiet but continuous growth of HEW agencies—particularly the Social Security Administration and the National Institutes of Health. His years were punctuated, however, by two controversial episodes that provide insight into the kind of problems that all HEW secretaries have faced.

The first episode began with Flemming's discovery, during a trip to the Northwest four weeks before Thanksgiving in 1959, that part of the nation's cranberry crop was contaminated by the pesticide spray aminotriazole. A year before, after tests on laboratory animals showed that in large amounts aminotriazole could cause cancer, Congress had made illegal the sale of food containing even the smallest trace of the chemical. After Flemming learned about the contamination, his first step was to call a press conference to alert the American people to the danger and to assure them that the FDA would confiscate all tainted shipments. But during the course of the press conference, a question emerged: How could consumers be sure they were getting pesticide-free cranberries when only lab tests could detect contamination? In the ensuing days, the public drastically reduced its purchase of cranberries. For the growers and distributors of cranberries, who normally made a good portion of their annual sales during the holiday season, this was catastrophic.

Flemming realized that in order to stave off consumer panic and save growers from financial ruin, his department had to take further action. An HEW-sponsored public hearing, at which experts assured the audience that a person had to eat almost a ton of fruit tainted with aminotriazole to be affected, helped to allay concern. But Flemming and his aides knew that the only way to restore consumer confidence completely would be to set up an emergency testing system to examine as much of the crop as possible. All of the FDA's laboratories, as well as some affiliated private facilities, were mobilized for the project. The media assisted in the campaign with regular bulletins telling consumers which batches of cranberries had been certified by the FDA. Ultimately, however, the public was not sufficiently reassured. The majority of cranberries went unsold and most growers—both those who had used the dangerous pesticide and those who had not—incurred steep losses.

The second episode involved a law passed by the Louisiana legislature in the spring of 1960 that declared "unsuitable families"—in other words, families with illegitimate children—as ineligible for benefits from the federally funded, state-administered public assistance program for families with dependent children. Flemming and officials at the Social Security Administration's Bureau of Public Assistance—the federal agency that oversaw the Aid to Families with Dependent Children program—were not pleased. But they had few grounds on which to act because the Social Security Administration had tolerated the passage of similar laws in other states. The difference in this instance was that Louisiana officials planned to apply the statute to *all* families with illegitimate children, whereas other states had applied it on a limited, case-by-case basis.

When the law took effect on July 1, 1960, aid was immediately cut off from thousands of families, most of whom had few other resources upon which to draw. Many families were reduced to begging. The issue gained national attention when the *Washington Post* ran a story detailing the desperate conditions in which the families lived. Disturbed by the adverse publicity his department had received from the story, Flemming dispatched SSA commissioner William Mitchell to Louisiana to try to convince leaders there to take responsibility for illegitimate children. To Flemming, it seemed extremely unfair that children should be punished for the indiscretions of their parents. Eventually, Mitchell convinced Louisiana to end its policy of summarily cutting off aid to all "unsuitable" families and instead to apply the law on a case-by-case basis. Flemming was not satisfied, however. He wanted to go further and establish a regulation making invalid all laws like the one in Louisiana. Over the

The owners of a New Jersey cannery are surrounded by thousands of containers of cranberry sauce that went unsold during the 1959 holiday season as a result of HEW's announcement that part of the nation's cranberry crop was contaminated by a potentially harmful pesticide.

objections of his general counsel, who believed the secretary was overstepping his authority, Flemming issued such a regulation on January 17, 1960, three days before the end of his term.

The Hand of Hope

When John F. Kennedy took office as president in 1960, it was a time of general prosperity. Nevertheless, a minority of the population—especially but not exclusively a black minority—was not sharing in the general affluence. In his inaugural address, Kennedy asked the nation "to bear the burden of a long twilight struggle against the common diseases of man: tyranny, poverty, disease, and war." He insisted that "the hand of hope must be extended to the

With HEW Secretary Abraham Ribicoff (far left) looking on, President John F. Kennedy (far right) welcomes the 15 millionth recipient of Social Security and his wife to the White House. Throughout his presidency, Kennedy worked to spread awareness of disadvantaged groups such as the aged.

poor and the depressed." Kennedy's speech helped to instill in Americans an increased concern for the disinherited and an increased interest in social action.

Over the course of his presidency, other factors helped increase the nation's awareness of the poor. Many Americans came to realize that poverty was an embarrassment that gave the Soviet Union ammunition to use against the United States in the cold war. In addition, newspapers spread information about the plight of poor urban residents, including blacks, Mexican Americans, Puerto Ricans, and American Indians. Because of the mechanization of agriculture, many members of these groups had moved to the cities during the 1950s and 1960s. (New machines and agricultural methods reduced farm employment by 45 percent between 1940 and 1970.) But with factory employment also on the decline, there were few opportunities for these new urban dwellers and most of them were forced to live in depressing slums and to seek public assistance from the government.

The civil rights movement and several important academic studies also helped spread awareness of poverty. The historian Gabriel Kulko, in his book *Wealth and Power in America*, and James Morgan, in *Income and Welfare in the United States*, argued that contrary to the belief of many Americans, the New Deal and World War II had not eliminated poverty. Sociologist Michael Harrington, in his book *The Other America*, described the impoverished as "a hidden subculture, one that was beyond the reach of the contemporary welfare state, one that perpetuated itself in an endless cycle." Over the course of the 1960s, increased concern for the poor led to the creation of hundreds of new social-service, income-maintenance, job-training, and public-health programs— the vast majority of which were assigned to HEW. Many of these programs were conceived by the Kennedy administration, but it would be left to his successor to steer them through Congress.

Kennedy appointed Abraham Ribicoff, the governor of Connecticut, as secretary of HEW. As his principal aide, Ribicoff chose Wilbur Cohen, who had helped draft the original Social Security Act and then had served for several years in the Social Security Administration. At the outset, Ribicoff and Cohen dedicated most of their energy to seeking changes in the Social Security Act to improve the Aid to Families with Dependent Children program.

As it stood, the program provided funds only to families in which one parent was either absent from the home or dead. It did not supply assistance to families in which both parents were present, even if both were unemployed. Hence, there was a great deal of incentive for poor, two-parent families to have one of the parents leave home. Though the program intended to strengthen families by providing financial support, in fact it led to the breakup of many.

61

With Kennedy's blessing, Ribicoff and Cohen sought to extend coverage to two-parent families in which the principal earner was unemployed. After more than a year of lobbying, they convinced Congress to do so by passing the Public Welfare Amendments of 1962. Unfortunately, the bill did not *require* states to grant coverage to unemployed parents, but merely gave them the option of doing so. By 1972, only 22 states had exercised that option.

Casting a shadow over Ribicoff's entire term in office was the nagging question of whether HEW should take a more active role in enforcing the Supreme Court's 1954 decision in the case *Brown v. the Board of Education of Topeka, Kansas.* That landmark ruling had called for the desegregation of American schools with "all deliberate speed." Many liberal lawmakers, led by Adam Clayton Powell, Jr., the vocal black congressman from Harlem, urged HEW to use its control over federal funds for education to force schools to desegregate. But ultimately, Ribicoff chose not to pursue such a strategy because it would have entailed withholding substantial funds from southern states, whose Democrats had provided invaluable support to Kennedy in the 1960 election.

Toward the end of his tenure, Ribicoff introduced a number of new HEW programs in response to events on the international scene. Amid rising concern about the possibility of nuclear attack on the United States, HEW assisted the Department of Agriculture in stockpiling medical supplies and food for fallout shelters. HEW also provided education, housing, and financial assistance for the 60,000 men and women who came to the United States after fleeing Fidel Castro's communist regime in Cuba. In spite of some impressive accomplishments, Ribicoff decided after a year and a half in office that his job was an impossible one. In July 1962, he resigned in order to run for the U.S. Senate. In a solemn press conference, he described the programs of HEW as too numerous and diverse to be managed by a single department.

As Ribicoff's replacement Kennedy chose a newcomer to the federal government, Anthony Celebrezze, an Italian-born politician who was in his fifth term as mayor of Cleveland. Celebrezze renewed efforts begun under Ribicoff to improve federal public assistance, or welfare, programs—which then consisted of income subsidies to the blind, the aged, and poor families with children. At the time these programs, though they involved the allocation of $4 billion a year in welfare grants to the states, were all administered by the Social Security Administration's Bureau of Public Assistance, which had only 375 employees. Celebrezze decided that a much larger, more influential agency should be responsible for such important programs. On January 25, 1963, he created the Welfare Administration—an agency with the same status as the

Underprivileged youths idle the day away on the streets of Harlem, in New York City. In 1962, at HEW Secretary Ribicoff's urging, Congress expanded the federal assistance program for poor families with dependent children.

Social Security Administration—and transferred to it responsibility for all public-assistance programs. The new agency also took over management of the Children's Bureau, the Cuban Refugee Program, the Office of Juvenile Delinquency, and the child health and welfare programs created by the 1935 Social Security Act.

The War on Poverty

In November 1963, a little more than a year after Celebrezze took office, President Kennedy was shot and killed in Dallas, Texas. His successor, Lyndon B. Johnson, renewed and intensified Kennedy's campaign against poverty. Johnson believed that unemployment, inadequate schools, juvenile

63

delinquency, and urban squalor had reached disastrous proportions. In his 1964 State of the Union address, he called upon Congress to enact a 13-point program that would declare "unconditional war on poverty, a drastic enemy which threatens the strength of our nation and the welfare of our people." (At the time of the speech, about 20 percent of the American people lived in poverty, including nearly half of the nation's blacks.) Lawmakers reacted enthusiastically to Johnson's proposal. For some, this reflected a desire to demonstrate national unity in the wake of the tragic death of President Kennedy. Others had made up their mind to seek remedies for poverty after witnessing the 1963 march on Washington, in which more than 250,000 people gathered in the capital to demand a civil rights bill and a jobs program.

Seven months after Johnson's address, a period of furious legislative activity began with the passage of the Economic Opportunity Act (EOA). As the centerpiece of Johnson's so-called War on Poverty, the bill provided for a wide array of social services, including a Jobs Corps to train young people who were chronically unemployed; literacy programs to teach English to illiterate adults; a Neighborhood Youth Corps to provide jobs for unemployed teenagers; and Operation Head Start, a project to give preschool education to poor children. A new agency called the Office of Economic Opportunity was established to administer the act, but HEW provided assistance to several of the new programs and in later years assumed full responsibility for many of them.

Later in 1964 and in 1965, Congress passed a flurry of other social-welfare bills that had a more immediate impact on HEW. Under the 1964 Civil Rights Act, which prohibited discrimination in the use of federal funds, HEW set up its Office of Civil Rights to make sure that none of the department's grants for education, health, and social-service programs went to organizations that refused to serve minority groups. The Elementary and Secondary Education Act and the Higher Education Act, passed by Congress in 1965, significantly increased federal aid to schools, particularly those that served disadvantaged groups. Put in charge of administering these laws, the Office of Education saw its budget rise from $1.5 billion in 1965 to $3.4 billion in 1966. Under the Older Americans Act of 1965, HEW set up the Administration on Aging to distribute grants to the states for education, health, transportation, community centers, in-home care, and other social services for the aged.

The Johnson administration also won passage of several bills that expanded the duties of the Public Health Service. The Health Professions Educational Assistance Act authorized a new program of federal grants to help build schools for the training of health professionals. In addition, it established a tuition loan program for medical and dental students. The Nurse Training Act authorized

Nearly a quarter million Americans marched on Washington, D.C., in August 1963 to demand increased federal attention to poverty and civil rights. The demonstration helped President Lyndon B. Johnson convince Congress to establish a wide variety of antipoverty programs in 1964.

SURGEON GENERAL'S WARNING: Smoking
Causes Lung Cancer, Heart Disease,
Emphysema, And May Complicate Pregnancy.

SURGEON GENERAL'S WARNING: Quitting Smoking
Now Greatly Reduces Serious Risks to Your Health.

SURGEON GENERAL'S WARNING: Smoking
By Pregnant Women May Result in Fetal Injury,
Premature Birth, And Low Birth Weight.

SURGEON GENERAL'S WARNING: Cigarette
Smoke Contains Carbon Monoxide.

Since the passage of the Federal Ciga-rette Labels and Ad-vertising Act in 1966, cigarette man-ufacturers have been required to dis-play health warn-ings on all packages and advertisements. The Public Health Service is charged with enforcing the act.

federal aid for construction and rehabilitation of nursing schools and established a loan fund for student nurses. After the surgeon general published a report in 1964 declaring that smoking might be hazardous to a person's health, Congress passed the Federal Cigarette Labels and Advertising Act, which required cigarette manufacturers to provide warnings on cigarette packages and advertisements about the dangers of smoking. The PHS was asked to enforce the law.

During Johnson's presidency, HEW initiated federal efforts to control air pollution. Under the Clean Air Act of 1963, the department provided federal grants to local air pollution agencies and dealt with interstate air pollution problems. In 1965, Congress asked the HEW secretary to establish nationwide exhaust-emission standards for new motor vehicles. The first such standards, issued in 1966, helped convince automakers to begin developing engines that used low-pollution unleaded gasoline.

The Creation of Medicare and Medicaid

In the summer of 1965, toward the end of Celebrezze's term as secretary of HEW, Congress passed legislation establishing the first major federal medical-insurance programs. It had been a long time in coming. The idea had been tossed around Washington since Roosevelt's Committee on Economic Security drew up plans for Social Security in 1934. Over the years, Democratic presidents had usually supported it, Republican chief executives had opposed it, and lawmakers had been undecided. By the time Kennedy took office, most members of the House had come out in support of medical insurance, but the House Ways and Means Committee and its powerful chairman Wilbur Mills, a conservative from Arkansas, opposed it. (For a medical insurance plan to come

Smog engulfs west Los Angeles. During the mid-1960s, HEW initiated the first federal efforts to control air pollution, administering grants to local pollution control agencies and establishing exhaust-emission standards for new motor vehicles.

up for a vote in the House, it first had to receive approval from Mills' committee.) Mills changed his mind, however, after the 1964 election increased liberal representation on the Ways and Means Committee, ensuring that a majority of panel members would approve medical insurance no matter how Mills voted.

In early 1965, Mills worked with members of Johnson's staff to draft a medical-insurance bill. In an attempt to reassure lawmakers worried about the cost, the scope of the bill was kept extremely limited. Only aged recipients of Social Security would be eligible, an arrangement that could easily be paid for

With Vice-president Hubert Humphrey (center) and former president Harry S. Truman (right) noting the time of the historic event, President Johnson signs the 1965 Medicare Act, which established federal medical insurance for the aged and the poor. HEW was assigned to administer the programs.

with excess Social Security funds. The plan, which was called Medicare, would cover only hospital expenses, not doctors' bills. This last provision was meant to appease doctors who belonged to the American Medical Association, and who were convinced that the creation of government insurance to cover doctors' bills would subject them to extensive federal regulation. When Mills' bill came before the Ways and Means Committee, it was expanded to include not just doctors' insurance (which covered doctors' bills), but also a separate, federally funded, state-administered medical insurance plan for the poor called Medicaid. In late July 1965, Medicaid and both parts of Medicare were approved by Congress.

Between 1962 and 1966 Congress passed several other bills that increased HEW's duties, including the Mental Retardation Facilities and Community Mental Health Construction Act (1963), the Maternal and Child Health Amendments (1963), and the Drug Abuse Control Amendments (1965). In all, HEW took over responsibility for 60 new programs during Celebrezze's 3 years in office, bringing the total number of programs handled by the department to 210. This resulted in phenomenal growth for HEW.

Like most other HEW secretaries, Celebrezze endured a fair amount of controversy. Under his direction, the department began providing birth-control information and funding the distribution of contraceptives, prompting vehement protests from religious leaders and conservative congressmen. A similar outcry greeted Celebrezze's decision to ban the use of krebiozen, a drug that supposedly helped to cure cancer.

In August 1965, Celebrezze accepted an appointment as a federal judge and was replaced as HEW secretary by John Gardner, an educator, writer, and psychologist. Gardner focused primarily on strengthening the department's organization. In November 1965, he announced a proposal to alter HEW's structure to resemble that of the Department of Defense—a so-called superdepartment (that is, it was divided into several subcabinet departments, each of which was headed by a secretary). But Johnson's advisers rejected the proposal, arguing that it would give too much authority to division heads, encouraging "separatism" and "empire building." Despite the failure of this plan, Gardner found other ways to modify HEW's organization to suit its many new responsibilities. He enlarged the secretary's staff, hired HEW's first planning and program-evaluation experts, and separated financial and nonfinancial management. He also created the new post of special assistant to the secretary for civil rights to ensure that programs funded by HEW complied with the Civil Rights Act.

In early 1968, Gardner mysteriously resigned from office with no explanation and was succeeded by HEW under secretary Wilbur Cohen, who had been Secretary Ribicoff's chief aide during the early 1960s. Serving under a lame-duck president, Cohen had little opportunity to launch new programs but he did conduct an important reorganization of the Public Health Service. Since its establishment as an official government agency in 1870, the PHS had been headed by the surgeon general, a position filled by career personnel from the Commissioned Corps. Cohen believed that career officers, while competent managers, were not adept at developing innovative policies. On March 13, 1968, Cohen transferred authority over the PHS to an official who he thought would be more capable of creative policy development, the assistant secretary for health and scientific affairs. Until that time, the assistant secretary had served as an adviser to the HEW secretary but had not been involved in program direction. The surgeon general was demoted to the second spot in the PHS, receiving the rank of deputy assistant secretary. Needless to say, the change was not well received by members of the Commissioned Corps. Cohen also overhauled the PHS's structure, setting up three basic subdivisions—the FDA, the NIH, and the Health Services and Mental Health Administration (HSMHA).

Assessing the War on Poverty

By 1968, the boom in social legislation had ended. On the whole, Johnson's social programs had produced limited results. On the one hand, inadequate funding had turned the Economic Opportunity Act "from a war on poverty into a minor skirmish," in the words of historian Walter Trattner. The total funds allotted to the program each year would not have solved the welfare problems of a single city. Toward the end of his presidency, Johnson began dismantling the Office of Economic Opportunity. The failure of the program to deliver what it had promised discouraged the poor, helping to bring about vicious urban riots during the late 1960s. Many liberals were forced to question the value of social activism. On the other hand, Medicare had enabled many older people to afford medical care they otherwise would not have received. Medicaid had enabled many poor people to escape dependence on overcrowded public medical facilities. And federal programs that provided job training, job placement, education, and public assistance to disadvantaged groups had helped reduce the number of Americans below the poverty level by nearly 50 percent between 1960 and 1968.

Workers board up a condemned government housing project in Dallas, Texas, during the late 1960s. In its attempt to resuscitate urban ghettos, Johnson's War on Poverty had limited success, but it did reduce by 50 percent the number of people living below the poverty line.

The War on Poverty was least effective in the area of welfare reform. In spite of such bills as the Public Welfare Amendments of 1962, during the Kennedy and Johnson years the number of recipients of Aid to Families with Dependent Children had increased by more than 60 percent. The cost of the program had more than doubled. There had been frequent reports of families lying about their income in order to qualify for assistance. Many Americans were uncomfortable with the idea of welfare benefits supporting women who were unwed or had been deserted by their husbands. Conservatives charged that welfare programs encouraged laziness and immorality. The attitude of many Americans was perhaps best captured by Senator Russell Long of Louisiana, who asserted that the "welfare system is being manipulated and abused by manipulators, cheats, and frauds." By the late 1960s, a full-fledged backlash against welfare had developed, which culminated in Congress's imposition of a ceiling on the number of families that could receive AFDC.

The Nixon Years: Stemming the Growth of Social Welfare

By the time of the 1968 presidential election, the "welfare mess," the decade's social turmoil, and the failure of War on Poverty programs had combined to turn many Americans against extensive federal involvement in social welfare. Members of the middle class had come to resent the attention paid to the poor, believing that while billions of dollars were being poured into the ghettos, the interests of "hardworking" citizens were being ignored. The Republican candidate, Richard M. Nixon, capitalized on this mood to win a resounding victory in the election. He presented himself as dedicated to traditional values, outspokenly critical of federal involvement in social services, suspicious of bureaucrats, and antagonistic to welfare. Conservative voters expected that Nixon would reduce government services and expenditures.

Once in office, Nixon did begin moving the country in this direction. He launched a series of programs, called the New Federalism, that attempted, in his words, "to reverse the flow of power and resources from the states and communities to Washington and to start power and resources flowing back to people all across America." He slashed the budgets of many social-service programs enacted earlier in the 1960s. On several occasions, he impounded funds intended for community health centers. And in 1970, he vetoed the HEW budget as too inflationary. But overall, Nixon did not attack the welfare state nearly as vigorously as many of his conservative supporters had urged. He left the majority of social programs intact and established several new ones.

For its part, HEW continued its relentless growth. HEW programs for children were expanded considerably. An Office of Child Development was set up in the secretary's office to coordinate various HEW activities that benefited children. The office took over management of the Children's Bureau and the Head Start program, which was transferred from the Office of Economic Opportunity. On October 29, 1969, the department set up the National Center for Family Planning, which was to provide disadvantaged women with family planning services, including counseling and birth control.

A number of laws passed by Congress enlarged the department's duties in other areas. The Older Americans Act of 1969 gave the HEW's Administration on Aging increased funds to distribute to the states for programs for the elderly. The Migrant Health Amendments Act granted money to the PHS to provide medical services for migrant farm workers. The Community Mental Centers Amendments established funding for community mental-health services for poor people. And amendments to the Social Security Act increased benefits for recipients of old-age, disability, and survivors' insurance.

In 1972, responsibility for administering the federally funded public-assistance programs for the blind, disabled, and the aged was transferred from the states to the Social Security Administration, and the programs were consolidated as the Supplemental Security Income program. The Child Abuse Prevention and Treatment Act of 1974 gave HEW authority to disburse federal funds to state programs combating child abuse.

The Nixon years witnessed particular growth in the Public Health Service. In 1970, the NIH added the National Institute on Alcohol Abuse and Alcoholism and the National Institute for Occupational Safety and Health. That same year, the PHS set up the National Health Service Corps to place physicians and other health professionals in areas with critical shortages of health employees. In 1972, Congress increased funding to the National Cancer Institute, enabling it to spearhead a national campaign against cancer. And in 1973, the PHS was expanded from three to five divisions. The FDA and NIH were kept intact, but the HSMHA was divided into the Health Resources Administration and the Health Services Administration. A fifth division, the Centers for Disease Control, was set up in Atlanta, Georgia, to prevent and control infectious diseases, to respond to public health emergencies, and to promote health through education and information. In 1974, a sixth division, the Alcohol, Drug Abuse, and Mental Health Administration, was added.

Daniel Patrick Moynihan (second from right) is sworn in as ambassador to the United Nations in 1975. Earlier in his career, as urban affairs adviser to President Nixon, Moynihan had proposed a radical plan to replace existing welfare programs with a federally guaranteed minimum income.

Nixon surprised many people with his approach to welfare reform. For many years, welfare critics of all political orientations had objected to the fact that under AFDC, intact poor families—that is, those with a mother and father both present in the home—were often excluded from assistance, even though their income might be lower than that of single-parent families who were eligible for welfare payments. At the urging of his urban affairs adviser, Daniel Patrick Moynihan, in August 1969 President Nixon proposed replacing AFDC with a "guaranteed annual income" or "negative income tax."

Under the proposed plan, called the Family Assistance Plan (FAP), any family whose income fell below a certain level would automatically receive benefits—whether or not one or both parents worked, and whether or not they were present in the home. Every poor family with children would receive at least $1,600 in federal money each year. But to keep people from relying indefinitely on those payments, the program would require each beneficiary to have a job or be enrolled in a job training program. The recipients who worked would be allowed to keep benefits until their annual total income rose above $4,000.

The proposal was radical in that it planned to give benefits to all the poor, not just to the disabled, retired, or unemployed, but it appealed to conservatives in Congress because it seemed to provide strong incentives for welfare recipients to find jobs and seemed likely to reduce welfare cheating. After receiving the blessing of Wilbur Mills and other conservatives, the FAP passed in the House. In the Senate, however, the bill was opposed both by conservatives, who argued that it would cost too much, and by liberals, who thought benefit levels were not high enough and were wary of any social legislation recommended by a Republican. After several years of discussion, the bill died in committee.

Nixon's HEW Secretaries

As representatives of a party that was often hostile to social-welfare programs, the three men who served as secretary of HEW under Nixon were in a difficult position. On the one hand, they were under pressure from the Republican president to carry out substantial changes—and often reductions—in department programs. On the other hand, they were forced to solicit the assistance of career personnel who were highly resistant to change.

All three of Nixon's HEW secretaries endured a fair amount of controversy. Under the first, Robert H. Finch, the former lieutenant governor of California, the department was plagued by internal conflict and public criticism. Soon after Finch took office, a group of 2,000 HEW employees presented him with a petition charging that President Nixon was not sufficiently committed to enforcement of the Civil Rights Act. Other HEW staffers expressed opposition to Nixon's slowness in withdrawing the United States from the Vietnam War. In 1969, the department was damaged by the revelation that for many years it had maintained a blacklist of doctors and scientists who were not eligible to receive NIH research grants. The group included a Nobel laureate in physics. Like many previous secretaries, Finch incurred the wrath of the business community by vigorously applying the FDA's regulatory powers. He prohibited the sale of a class of artificial sweeteners called cyclamates and, in cooperation with the Department of Agriculture, he phased out the pesticide DDT. Finch further alienated big business by establishing strict guidelines for industrial air-pollution control. These guidelines specified maximum levels of sulfur dioxide and total suspended particulates that could be emitted from industrial plants. (In 1970, the Environmental Protection Agency assumed responsibility for enforcing these guidelines and took over all of HEW's other duties in the area of air pollution control.) By June 1970, Nixon had become disenchanted with Finch's performance, particularly by his inability to quiet the rabble-rousers inside the department, and he moved the HEW secretary to the Executive Office of the President.

Finch's replacement, Elliott Richardson, came to the office better prepared than any previous HEW secretary. He had worked in all three branches of

President Richard M. Nixon meets with Caspar Weinberger, who served as HEW secretary from 1973 to 1975. With Weinberger's help, Nixon cut funding for many social programs. Nevertheless, HEW continued to grow.

government—legislative, executive, and judicial—and had gained experience on both the state and federal levels. Shortly after being sworn in, Richardson delivered a memorable speech to HEW employees, outlining his basic social philosophy. Called "Responsibility and Responsiveness," the speech urged HEW divisions to set realistic goals so as not to raise unfairly the expectations of the poor. He called for an emphasis on "prevention of dependency and the accomplishment of institutional reform." The speech improved department morale enormously. Nevertheless, criticism of HEW by Congress and the public continued. During Richardson's tenure, the National Institutes of Health were sued by women's groups for discriminatory practices. Congress looked into charges that officials of the FDA's Division of Biological Standards had taken bribes from drug manufacturers in exchange for leniency in product inspection. And the Public Health Service drew fire from the scientific community for dismissing several well-respected officials.

After Nixon's reelection in 1972, Richardson was shifted to the more prestigious post of secretary of defense and was succeeded by Caspar Weinberger. A native of California, Weinberger had served as chairman of the Federal Trade Commission and director of the Office of Management and Budget during Nixon's first term. (He later would serve as secretary of defense under President Ronald Reagan.) As secretary of HEW, Weinberger made several important organizational changes. He established the position of assistant secretary for human development to coordinate the Office of Child Development, the Administration on Aging, and most of HEW's social-service programs. (In 1980, when the Office of Human Development Services was established as one of HHS's four main divisions, this assistant secretary was put in charge of it.) Weinberger transferred many of his own day-to-day administrative duties to the under secretary, Frank Carlucci. He also played a key role in the 1973 expansion of the Public Health Service.

Ford and Carter: The Retreat Continues

Two and a half years into Weinberger's term, Nixon resigned from office amid revelations that his reelection committee had committed several illegal acts—including bugging and breaking into a Democratic party office in the Watergate Hotel in Washington, D.C. His successor, Gerald Ford, was even more antagonistic toward social-welfare programs than Nixon had been. Several major welfare bills—including proposals for a new school lunch program, a public-works project, and increased spending for education and health—were struck down by the president's veto. Ford also vehemently opposed attempts to expand federal medical insurance and on several occasions slashed HEW's budget. Not a single proposal to aid the needy emerged from his office. Meanwhile, the number of poor people increased dramatically. In 1975, the unemployment rate rose to nine percent, the highest rate since 1941. In the same year, the number of Americans below the poverty level—which had remained constant at about 25 million from 1969 to 1974—suddenly jumped by 2.5 million.

Like his predecessors, Ford's HEW secretary, F. David Matthews, had the difficult job of directing a department toward which the president was often hostile. An academic who had served as president of the University of Alabama and had written several books on southern history, Matthews spent a great deal of his time trying to improve the department's educational programs. He also launched an HEW program to combat lead poisoning and stepped up the department's efforts to curb drug abuse. In response to charges that HEW officials had embezzled funds meant for loans to students, Matthews set up the position of inspector general.

In 1976, Jimmy Carter, the little-known Democratic governor of Georgia, capitalized on the American people's dissatisfaction with Ford's handling of the economy and the post-Watergate distrust of career politicians to win the presidency. Carter believed, as many Americans did, that the federal government should recognize limits to its power and exercise restraint in funding new programs. At the same time, as an old-fashioned populist (supporter of the common people), he was determined to reverse the trend toward dismantling the welfare state begun by Nixon.

In his first months in office, Carter proposed an extensive agenda of social legislation. On August 6, 1977, he proposed a plan to reform the welfare system. Called the Better Jobs and Income Program (BJIP), the plan would have replaced the confusing array of federal public-assistance programs—including the SSI and AFDC—with a single system composed of two parts: a job program for those who could work and income subsidies for those who could not. All poor people—whether or not they were employed or had families—would have received a guaranteed minimum income. The proposal was defeated in Congress, however, by a coalition of conservatives who were disturbed by its expense, and liberals who thought the plan was too similar to Nixon's FAP. In May 1977, Carter proposed to enlarge the Social Security trust fund—the financial integrity of which had been threatened by rising unemployment and inflation—by using funds from general revenue. This measure was also killed by lawmakers, who chose instead to replenish Social Security by increasing taxes on workers' paychecks.

In July 1978, Carter proposed an expansion of federal medical insurance called Health Care. This too was defeated, primarily because many perennial advocates of universal health insurance, such as Senator Edward Kennedy of

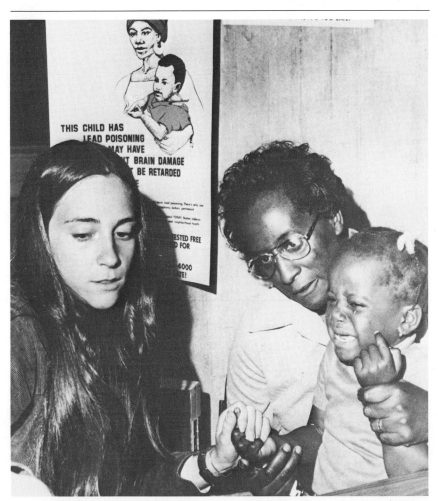

A social worker (left) tests a four-year-old child for lead poisoning at a clinic in Boston. The federal government launched a program to combat lead poisoning under President Gerald Ford's HEW secretary, F. David Matthews.

Massachusetts, thought its coverage was too limited. Carter did manage to secure passage of several important manpower programs. But ultimately, the vast majority of his proposals in the area of social welfare were defeated by Congress, in spite of the Democratic party's control of both houses. In large part, these failures resulted from Carter's inability to ingratiate himself with Democratic leaders in Congress.

In 1977, Carter appointed Joseph A. Califano, a lawyer and special assistant to the secretary of defense, as secretary of HEW. During Califano's tenure, the department faced charges of fraud and mismanagement. One member of the president's staff claimed that five percent of HEW's 1977 budget was eaten up by embezzlement and inefficiency. In 1978, 15 former and current HEW officials were indicted by a grand jury for fraud. Califano engendered further controversy by stringently enforcing minority quotas in hiring new HEW employees, by endorsing several antismoking bills, and by ordering NIH researchers to investigate the possibility that the government's testing of

In 1977–78, HEW secretary Joseph Califano (left) and President Jimmy Carter (right) attempted to increase Social Security benefits, expand federal medical insurance, and establish several new social programs. Most of their proposals were rejected by Congress.

An atomic bomb explodes over the Pacific Ocean in a test conducted by the United States government. In 1977, Secretary Califano ordered HEW medical researchers to investigate the possibility that nuclear weapons tests had caused cancer in residents of western states.

atomic bombs in Utah, New Mexico, and Nevada during the 1940s and 1950s had caused some residents of those states to develop cancer. Almost from the day he was appointed, Califano had difficulty getting along with Carter. The president was disturbed by the secretary's close relationship with Edward Kennedy, Carter's nemesis in Congress, and blamed Califano for the failure of the welfare and medical-insurance bills. In 1979, Califano was dismissed and replaced by Patricia Harris, the former dean of Howard University's law school and the secretary of housing and urban development from 1977 to 1979.

Under the last HEW secretary, Patricia Harris (shown here address-ing a steelworkers' convention), the department was reorganized in 1979. The Office of Education was made a separate, cabinet-level de-partment and the rest of HEW became the Department of Health and Human Services (HHS). Harris was sworn in as the first HHS secre-tary in 1980.

FIVE

HHS:
Target of the
Reagan Revolution

Almost since the Office of Education was established in 1867, educators had urged Congress to give it cabinet-level status. During Lyndon Johnson's presidency, three temporary executive panels had investigated the idea. By the time Jimmy Carter faced off against Gerald Ford in the 1976 presidential election, advocates of a cabinet-level education department had gained considerable strength. The National Education Association (NEA), a teachers' union and lobbying group, had accumulated 1.8 million members and had become a major player in national politics. To secure the support of the NEA in his bid for the presidency, Carter had promised to represent its educational program once elected. In turn, the NEA agreed to do something it had never done before—endorse a presidential candidate. Once in office, Carter felt compelled to pursue the NEA's primary goal—the separation of the Office of Education from HEW to create a cabinet-level Department of Education.

The Division of HEW

In April 1977, Carter appointed a task force to draft a proposal for reorganizing HEW. There were many arguments for and against the division of the

24-year-old department. Proponents of a separate education department argued that it would ensure that the official with final authority over national education policy had extensive experience in teaching and academic administration; in many instances, HEW secretaries had come to the job knowing a great deal about welfare and social insurance and nothing about the nation's schools. Proponents also insisted that a cabinet-level education department would improve efficiency in education programs, give the president's education adviser greater visibility, and help convince federal leaders to pay more attention to improving the nation's school system.

On the other hand, many opponents of the proposal contended that education was not important enough to warrant the creation of a separate department. Others feared that a new department would lead to an overextension of the federal government's involvement in education and eventually threaten the rights of states to determine curricula. Still others—including HEW secretary Joseph Califano—argued that the desired improvements in federal education programs could be accomplished by simply reorganizing the existing Office of Education, without creating a new department. They warned that the proposed department would be taken over by the teachers' lobby. Even one teachers' union, the American Federation of Teachers, opposed the plan, fearing it would be dominated by its rival organization, the NEA.

All of these viewpoints were represented in Congress, which began discussions on a bill to establish a Department of Education in early 1978. When the bill came up for a vote later in the year, it was passed by the Senate but rejected by the House. In 1979, Carter renewed the effort to create an education department, waging an intense lobbying campaign. Once again, the bill passed easily in the Senate but faced stiff opposition in the House. This time, however, the House passed the bill by a slim margin. On October 17, 1979, President Carter signed the Department of Education Organization Act, which transferred HEW's education tasks to a new, cabinet-level Department of Education and established the cabinet-level Department of Health and Human Services to assume the remainder of HEW's duties.

After a 180-day transition period, both new departments opened their doors on May 4, 1980. HHS was given control over the vast majority of HEW's employees and most of its funds. The Department of Education was given only 17,000 employees and $14 billion from the HEW budget; HHS retained 140,000 staffers and a budget of $226 billion. Initially, HHS consisted of three main divisions—the Social Security Administration, the Public Health Service, and the Health Care Financing Administration, which Carter had established in 1977 to administer Medicare and Medicaid. It also contained a plethora of smaller bureaus that managed social-service programs. Soon after the department's reorganization, a fourth major division, the Office of Human Development Services, was created to consolidate most of HHS's social-service programs. In 1986, the Family Support Administration would be established to oversee social-service programs for families and the AFDC program, bringing the number of HHS divisions to its current total of five.

Patricia Harris, the last head of HEW, was kept on as the first secretary of HHS. During her eight months in the new post, she concentrated primarily on ironing out administrative problems that resulted from the reorganization. She was also called upon to represent the department in two controversies. The first resulted from the department's practice of granting Medicaid benefits to poor women who received abortions. In 1980, the Supreme Court put severe

Antiabortion marchers face off against a pro-choice demonstrator outside the office of a doctor who allegedly performed abortions. Foes of abortion won a major victory in 1980 when the Supreme Court ordered HHS to curtail its practice of funding abortions for poor women.

restrictions on this practice. Later in the year, Carter vetoed a bill that would have allotted funds to the NIH for investigation of the effects on humans of Agent Orange, a defoliant that was used extensively by American forces in the Vietnam War. Many Vietnam veterans claimed that exposure to Agent Orange had caused them to develop severe health problems ranging from skin diseases to cancer.

The Reagan Revolution

For Carter, the years 1979 and 1980 were a disaster. Islamic militants took over the American embassy in Iran in November 1979 and held its 52 occupants hostage. The president's inability to secure the hostages' release for more than a year and his halfhearted attempts to halt the Soviet occupation of Afghanistan contributed to the widespread perception that he was ineffectual and weak. His reputation was further damaged by the poor performance of the economy. In 1980, the inflation rate was in double digits and the unemployment rate, at 7.8 percent, was also high. That summer, Carter received the lowest approval rating ever recorded for an American president, 21 percent. Not surprisingly, the Republican candidate, Ronald Reagan, had little difficulty defeating Carter in the 1980 presidential election.

Reagan interpreted his victory not as a rejection of the incumbent, but as a mandate to institute drastic change. The changes Reagan envisioned reflected three basic ideals he had held since he was governor of California during the late 1960s and early 1970s: The federal government was too big, free enterprise and the success of big business were the keys to a healthy economy, and the military should be strengthened to deter attack by the "Evil Empire," the Soviet Union. In the area of economic policy, Reagan was a proponent of supply-side economics, or a blend of tax cuts, a balanced budget, reductions in government spending on social programs, and the liberation of industry from government regulation. The president's approach to social programs was largely based on the views of his domestic adviser, Martin Anderson, who had strongly criticized the War on Poverty in his book *Welfare*. Reagan was deeply suspicious of welfare recipients, believing that most of them were "cheats" or "freeloaders," and he proposed deep cuts in federal public-assistance benefits. As his long-range goal in social welfare, he sought to transfer responsibility for tending to the needy back to the states, local governments, churches, private foundations, fraternal groups, and charitable organizations. Returning to the pre–New Deal arrangement, he argued, was necessary because the federal government was incapable of administering social programs without waste and inefficiency.

Once in office, Reagan moved with swiftness and skill in putting his theories into practice. In only a few months, he was able to expand defense spending dramatically, to cut taxes (especially for the rich), and to slim down big government by cutting billions of dollars from the federal budget—mostly in the area of social welfare. Especially hard hit by the budget cuts were four HHS programs—the AFDC, SSI, Medicare, and Medicaid. In 1983 and 1984, President Reagan cut $125 billion from the federal budget for social programs.

Reagan had less success pursuing his long-term goal of transferring control of federal programs to the states. In his 1982 State of the Union address, Reagan asked Congress to give state officials full responsibility for funding and administering 46 federal programs, including AFDC, Medicaid, and all federal programs in the areas of special education, youth employment, job training, and mass transportation. Under the proposal, states would have been given the option of reducing the size of the programs or abolishing them altogether. But the proposal turned out to be extremely unpopular among both Republican and Democratic legislators and was never even discussed in committee.

Congress also headed off attempts by Reagan to cut funds for Social Security and in fact forced him to seek improvement in the social-insurance system. By the early 1980s, Social Security was badly in need of reform. An increase in the average life span of individuals, expansion of coverage to include new groups, and increases in payments to compensate for rises in the cost of living had combined to send the cost of retirement benefits soaring. At the same time, rising unemployment and a declining birthrate reduced the amount of money coming into the Social Security trust fund. In 1982, Reagan established the National Commission on Social Security Reform, a 15-member bipartisan panel headed by economist Alan Greenspan, to examine ways to revamp Social Security. The committee produced a rescue plan that drew almost unanimous support from both parties and also pleased the president. The plan promised to save $168 billion over the following 7 years by taking several steps: taxing the benefits of beneficiaries with an income greater than $25,000; introducing scheduled payroll-tax increases earlier than planned; gradually raising the retirement age from 65 to 67; and delaying an impending cost-of-living increase. The plan was approved by both houses of Congress and signed into law by President Reagan on April 20, 1983.

In 1981, Reagan appointed Richard Schweiker as secretary of HHS. A veteran of two terms in the Senate and five in the House, Schweiker was a devoted disciple of "Reaganomics." He assisted in the president's attempts to transfer control of HHS activities to the states and oversaw the dismantling and consolidation of many HHS programs. During his tenure, the department's staff was reduced from 169,000 employees to 128,000. In spite of his and Reagan's efforts, members of Congress and career HHS staffers fended off major cuts in the most essential HHS programs.

During his two years in office Schweiker weathered many controversies. In 1982, for instance, he came under attack from the Planned Parenthood Federation of America for introducing a proposal to require birth control centers to contact parents of underaged clients within 10 days of birth control purchases.

Over the course of the 1980s, the Public Health Service played an increasingly active role in efforts to control acquired immune deficiency syndrome (AIDS), a disease caused by a virus (HIV) that destroys the body's immune system, making it susceptible to a variety of cancers and infections.

During his unsuccessful bid for the presidency in 1976, Ronald Reagan (right) introduces a potential running mate, Richard Schweiker, to the press. After winning the 1980 election, Reagan named Schweiker as his HHS secretary and made drastic cuts in the budgets of several HHS programs, including Medicare and Medicaid.

Demonstrators in Washington, D.C., protest President Reagan's handling of the AIDS crisis. Under Reagan, the Public Health Service helped identify the disease and develop drugs to fight it, but many observers criticized the president for committing insufficient funds to AIDS research and education.

Epidemiologists for the Centers for Disease Control helped to identify the disease, define its symptoms, determine its causes, and chart its spread. The National Cancer Institute worked with pharmaceutical companies to develop the first clinically useful anti-AIDS drug, AZT. Inspectors for the FDA tested and approved the drug. And the surgeon general's office helped disseminate information on the dangers of AIDS and on ways to avoid contracting the disease.

The Public Health Service also helped expand public knowledge about the hazards of smoking. A 1986 report by the surgeon general about the effects of cigarette smoke on the health of nonsmokers helped spur many state and local efforts to ban smoking in public places. And in 1988, the surgeon general declared that nicotine in cigarettes was addictive, giving smokers ammunition in their fight to obtain damages from cigarette manufacturers.

Students at a Head Start center help their teacher prepare lunch.
The Head Start program—which provides needy preschool children
with education, health care, and counseling—is run by the Office of
Human Development Services, one of HHS's five operating divisions.

SIX

Today's Department

Today, in spite of the Reagan administration's assault on the welfare state, the Department of Health and Human Services remains a bureaucratic behemoth. It commands a budget that is larger than the gross national product of every foreign country except the Soviet Union. It is staffed by 120,000 employees. It is in charge of administering hundreds of pieces of legislation. It manages Social Security, Medicare, and Medicaid, conducts medical research, attempts to control contagious diseases, protects consumers against unsafe food and drugs, fights drug abuse, oversees the nation's hospitals, helps refugees settle in the United States, helps single parents collect unpaid child support, subsidizes home-energy costs, promotes economic development on Indian reservations, combats child abuse, safeguards the rights of the mentally retarded, runs shelters for runaway youths, and provides financial assistance to the poor—to name only some of its functions.

The Chain of Command

To carry out its myriad functions, HHS has dozens of bureaus and components, which are knit together in a structure as complex as that of any other government department in the world. At the top of the department's hierarchy is the secretary of health and human services. Because HHS is one of the executive branch's 14 senior departments, the secretary belongs to the cabinet, serving as the president's chief adviser on health, welfare, and income security programs. He or she also supervises the HHS staff in running the department's many programs.

The secretary is assisted in management tasks by the under secretary of health and human services, who serves as the second-in-command and takes over in emergencies; a deputy under secretary, who oversees relations with Congress and state and local governments; and the chief of staff. Because HHS is obliged to account for its use of taxpayers' money, all four of the department's top officials spend a lot of their time testifying before Congress, meeting with the press, making speeches before national organizations, and preparing regular reports required by law.

Beneath the four senior officials in HHS's pyramidal structure are eight offices that have staff functions. This means that they do not themselves carry out any HHS programs; instead they perform some function that helps the secretary to see that programs are carried out efficiently and properly. They

HEW Secretary Joseph Califano (left) and two other government officials appear before a congressional hearing on the Three Mile Island nuclear disaster. Like their HEW predecessors, HHS secretaries spend much of their time testifying before Congress and making speeches.

include the Office of Civil Rights and the offices of the general counsel, the inspector general, and five assistant secretaries—for management and budget, planning and evaluation, public affairs, personnel administration, and legislation.

The Office of the General Counsel furnishes legal advice to the secretary and other HHS officials. The Office of the Inspector General conducts routine audits and inspections of department programs to assess their effectiveness and identify their shortcomings. It also makes recommendations to the secretary on how to improve the efficiency of HHS activities and investigates charges of criminal activity, unethical conduct, and program abuse and fraud. The Office of Civil Rights ensures that state, local, and private institutions that receive HHS funds comply with Title VI of the 1964 Civil Rights Act, which prohibits discrimination on the basis of race, color, or national origin in programs receiving federal assistance.

The Office of the Assistant Secretary for Public Affairs handles relations with the media and prepares and distributes publications and audio materials that describe HHS's history and programs. The Office of the Assistant Secretary for Legislation draws up legislation that the HHS secretary wishes to propose, arranges for HHS officials to appear before congressional committees, and conducts regular briefings for members of Congress on HHS activities.

The Office of the Assistant Secretary for Planning and Evaluation develops the department's long-range social and economic policies and makes sure that its programs execute these policies. The Office of the Assistant Secretary for Personnel Administration oversees hiring, firing, promotion, and retirement of HHS employees, advises the HHS secretary on how to improve the quality of the department's staff, and attempts to increase the proportion of minority employees in the department. The Office of the Assistant Secretary for Management and Budget prepares the department's budget, coordinates financial management activities, and handles all administrative tasks aside from personnel supervision.

An additional office, the U.S. Office of Consumer Affairs, is situated within the HHS hierarchy on the level of the staff offices but reports directly to the president rather than to the HHS secretary. Headed by a special assistant to the president, the consumer office coordinates all federal programs that inform and protect the consumer and advises the president on consumer affairs.

Subordinate to the staff offices are HHS's five operating divisions, which have line functions—that is, they are responsible for actually carrying out the department's programs. These divisions are the Social Security Administration, the Health Care Financing Administration, the Office of Human Development Services, the Family Support Administration, and the Public Health Service.

The Social Security Administration

The Social Security Administration (SSA) is HHS's largest operating division, both in terms of budget and number of employees. It was established in 1935 as the Social Security Board to administer the social-insurance and public-assistance programs established by the Social Security Act. It was given its present name in 1946 after the three-member board that originally ran the agency was replaced by a single official, a commissioner. Over the years, it has taken on several new Social Security programs and relinquished others to different departments. In 1939, it added survivors' insurance, in 1956 disability insurance, and in 1965 Medicare and Medicaid. Meanwhile, in 1949 Unemployment Compensation was shifted to the Department of Labor, in 1963 Aid to Families with Dependent Children was shifted to the Welfare Administration, and in 1977 Medicare and Medicaid were shifted to the Health Care Financing Administration (HCFA). Today, the SSA is responsible for two programs, a social-insurance program called Social Security, or Old Age Survivors and Disability Insurance (OASDI), and a public-assistance program called Supplemental Security Income (SSI).

Social Security consists of three parts. Retirement insurance provides monthly payments to retired workers. Survivors' insurance provides monthly payments to the spouses and young children of deceased workers. Disability insurance provides monthly benefits to workers who are prevented from working for a year or longer by an illness or injury. All three types of benefits are paid out of a single trust fund that is maintained by assessing payroll taxes (called "contributions" by the government) on employers and employees. The size of the payment each beneficiary receives is determined by the amount of money he or she earned while working. Generally, the more a person earned, the more he or she receives in benefits—although workers at the lower end of the pay scale receive a higher percentage of their original income, because it is assumed they will have saved less money over the years. To pay people on this basis, the Social Security Administration keeps detailed records on the income of every worker—identifying each with a Social Security number.

The system works in the following manner: During each pay period, an employer deducts a worker's share of the Social Security tax from his or her wages. The employer adds a matching amount and sends a report to the Social Security Administration including the person's name and Social Security number and the total wages earned. All such reports are entered into the worker's Social Security record. This record is eventually used to determine the amount of benefits a person is owed. (For no charge, a worker may check

A Social Security Administration (SSA) official helps residents of a nursing home in Indiana sign up for Medicare in 1966. Medicare was administered by the SSA until 1977, when it was taken over by the Health Care Financing Administration.

his or her current Social Security record to make sure that wages have been tabulated correctly. In fact, the SSA recommends that records be checked every three years.)

In the early years of Social Security, many groups were excluded from coverage—farm laborers, farmers, domestic servants, clergymen, the self-employed, and employees of nonprofit organizations. But today, almost everyone is eligible regardless of occupation or income. In 1987, Social Security paid out more than $200 billion in benefits and served more than 38 million people. Around 61 percent of beneficiaries were retired workers, 7 percent were disabled, and 32 percent were spouses or children of retired, disabled, or deceased workers. Social Security is particularly important to the aged, providing at least 50 percent of total income to 62 percent of Americans 65 and over. It serves as the sole source of income for about a quarter of the elderly population.

The second SSA program, Supplemental Security Income, consists of cash payments to aged, blind, and disabled persons whose income falls below a certain amount. It is paid for by general tax revenues, rather than by a special trust fund.

The gargantuan tasks of issuing benefit payments and keeping records of workers' wages are handled primarily by the Social Security Administration's main office in Baltimore, Maryland. The agency also operates a network of 10 regional offices, 6 program service centers, and 1,300 local offices to provide a number of additional services. These offices help Americans understand the provisions and purposes of Social Security and SSI, help people file claims for benefits, help workers obtain wage records, and assist claimants in appealing decisions by the SSA regarding their benefits. A group of federal judges are assigned to the SSA to decide benefit appeals. But the SSA, through its Appeals Councils, has the power to make the final decision on any case.

Health Care Financing Administration

The Health Care Financing Administration (HCFA) was created in 1977 to take over management of the federal government's two medical insurance plans, Medicare and Medicaid. These had previously been overseen by the Social Security Administration.

Medicare is a medical insurance plan for people 65 years of age and older. It is also available to a small number of younger people—those who have been disabled for more than 24 months, those who need continuing dialysis for permanent kidney failure, and those who have received a kidney transplant. The program is funded by Social Security withholding taxes, fees paid by recipients, and general revenue, and is administered entirely by the federal government—unlike its sister program, Medicaid.

Medicare is divided into two parts. Hospital insurance (Part A) pays for inpatient hospital services, posthospital care at nursing homes, and hospice care for the terminally ill. (A hospice is a facility that attempts to fulfill the emotional and physical needs of the terminally ill.) Doctors insurance (Part B) covers physicians' services, outpatient hospital services, diagnostic tests, outpatient physical therapy, speech pathology services, medical equipment and supplies, and home-health services. Like most insurance programs, both of these plans require the patient to pay part of the bill. For Part A, the beneficiary is responsible for the first $520 incurred during each 60-day period; Medicare will pay for the rest. (This arrangement is referred to as a $520,

60-day deductible.) To receive Part B, Medicare recipients must pay a flat fee—called a premium—of $24.50 a month; the deductible for Part B is $75 a year. The HCFA does not itself handle claims; instead it hires private insurance companies, called intermediaries, to perform the task. Benefit payments for Part A are made directly to the health-care facility—that is, the hospital, nursing home, or physical therapy clinic. Payments for Part B may go either to the patient or the supplier—that is, the doctor, laboratory, or hospital. In fiscal year 1988, 32 million people received Medicare; benefit payments for that year totaled $70 billion.

Medicaid is a medical insurance plan for the poor. It is administered by the states, but the federal government pays part of the cost and establishes eligibility guidelines. The federal share of the cost varies from state to state but averages 57 percent. The states are obliged by federal law to provide Medicaid to recipients of Aid to Families with Dependent Children and recipients of Supplemental Security Income. At their discretion, states may also provide benefits to other groups. Almost half of the states assist people who are medically needy but whose income exceeds qualifications for welfare. Services for which states must provide benefits include doctor, hospital, and skilled-nursing home care; health screenings and follow-up treatment for children; laboratory and X-ray services for persons 21 and older; nurse-midwife services; home health-care services; family planning services; and rural health-clinic services. In 1987, 22 million people received Medicaid; benefit payments totaled $37 billion.

In addition to paying out benefits, the HCFA performs several other functions. It helps beneficiaries find out what services Medicare and Medicaid cover; it assists recipients in gaining access to services; and it tries to guarantee that recipients use benefit payments for the most effective and efficient services available. In recent years, national health-care costs have shot up dramatically, straining the HCFA's ability to pay all those entitled to medical insurance.

To prevent a crisis in health-care funding, the HCFA has taken four important steps. First, it is now urging health-care consumers to avoid, whenever possible, expensive overnight stays in hospitals in favor of less costly outpatient care. Second, the agency has agreed to fund several types of nontraditional care that are less expensive than hospitals: surgery centers, comprehensive rehabilitation facilities, and hospices. Third, it has changed the manner in which it reimburses hospitals. Whereas in the past hospitals were paid whatever they claimed to have spent on a patient (a system that was frequently abused), now they are paid preset rates on the basis of diagnosis.

Fourth, to reduce the incidence of unnecessary elective (nonemergency) surgery, the HCFA has launched a Second Opinion for Surgery Program, under which health-care consumers are encouraged to consult more than one physician when considering nonemergency surgery. Local HCFA referral centers provide patients with names of doctors and assistance in understanding medical terminology.

Office of Human Development Services

The Office of Human Development Services (HDS) administers all of HHS's social-service programs except for certain family-related programs that are handled by the Family Support Administration. The HDS's wide-ranging programs assist children, youths, families, the elderly, the poor, American Indians, the disabled, and persons living in rural areas. Established in 1980, HDS is headed by the assistant secretary for human development services. As the principal adviser to the secretary of HHS on social services, the assistant secretary helps coordinate social-service programs provided by the various components of HHS, other federal agencies, and state and local governments.

In recent years HDS has taken several steps to cope with reduced budgets for social services at the federal, state, and local levels. It has targeted federal funds for state and local social services that assist the neediest groups. It has developed methods for making social-service programs more cost-effective. And it has aided states in improving their management of social services. HDS contains four divisions: the Administration for Children, Youth, and Families, the Administration for Native Americans, the Administration on Aging, and the Administration on Developmental Disabilities.

Administration for Children, Youth, and Families (ACYF)

The ACYF administers and funds a panoply of social-service programs for children and families from every ethnic and geographic group. Primary emphasis is given to handicapped children, abused and neglected children, runaway youths, children and youths in need of adoption or other child-care services, children from low-income families, and children from Native American and migrant families. The agency came into being as the Office of Child Development in 1969, when the Children's Bureau and the Head Start program merged. It was given its present title in 1977 after adding child-welfare and youth programs. Currently it contains three major bureaus: the Children's Bureau, the Head Start Bureau, and the Family and Youth Services Bureau.

The Children's Bureau is the ACYF's oldest division. Established in 1912, it initially addressed such issues as child labor, maternal and child health, and juvenile delinquency. Today, it provides funds to states for child-welfare services (under a provision of the Social Security Act), helps find permanent homes for children adrift in the foster-care system, assists states and communities in planning adoption programs, and subsidizes undergraduate and graduate social-work schools that offer training in child and family services. To

Three generations of an impoverished American Indian family. The Administration for Native Americans, part of the Office of Human Development Service, tries to help Indians overcome chronic poverty by subsidizing economic development on reservations.

combat the pressing problem of child abuse—approximately 1.5 million children are victimized every year—the Children's Bureau operates the National Center for Child Abuse and Neglect, which serves as a national clearinghouse for information on child abuse.

Children from needy homes start life with certain disadvantages that make it extremely difficult for them to rise in society. Schools in poor neighborhoods usually offer them an inferior education. Inadequate nutrition and unstable home lives inhibit their intellectual and psychological development. To help counteract these disadvantages, the Head Start program was created in 1965. Directed by the Head Start Bureau, thousands of Head Start centers around the country provide needy children with free preschool education, health care, balanced meals, and counseling. Head Start officials also make a special effort to involve parents in the program as classroom assistants. In 1988, the program cost $1.2 billion and served 454,000 children.

The Family and Youth Services Bureau concentrates primarily on the problem of runaway and homeless youths. Each year, approximately 730,000 teenagers run away from or are forced out of their homes. To help these individuals, the bureau funds and coordinates a national network of youth shelters. The 315 facilities in the network provide temporary living accommodations, help reunite youths with their family, and place in alternative living situations those who cannot return home. The bureau also supports a national runaway hot line, which helps parents locate runaway children.

Also a part of HDS is the President's Council on Mental Retardation, a panel of 21 private citizens and 6 federal officials who help coordinate federal programs for mentally retarded people. Assisted by an executive director and a small staff, this committee devotes particular attention to assuring the civil and constitutional rights of America's 6 million retarded people and to reducing the incidence of mental retardation from biomedical and environmental causes.

Administration for Native Americans (ANA)

American Indians fare worse than any other ethnic group in the United States in almost every economic and health category. More than 14 percent of Indians who live on reservations make less than $2,000 yearly (the figure is 5 percent for the whole U.S. population). Only 6 percent earn $30,000 or more (compared with 20 percent for the United States as a whole). Reservation Indians have the highest rates of teenage suicide, alcoholism, and adult diabetes of any group in the country. The federal agency with primary responsibility for trying to help Indians overcome these problems is the Bureau

Senior citizens sit down to a free meal at a government-funded community center. The Administration on Aging administers grants to state and local agencies that provide senior center programs, legal counsel, in-home meals, and other services for senior citizens.

of Indian Affairs (BIA) in the Department of the Interior. But to supplement BIA activities in the area of social service programs, the ANA was set up in 1974.

Unlike the BIA, which deals primarily with reservation Indians, the ANA assists Indians both on and off reservations. Stated in general terms, the ANA's goals are to promote Indian economic and social development and to encourage tribes to assume increased responsibility for their own affairs. Specifically, the ANA provides to Native American tribal governments and other Native American organizations funds to help tribes create jobs, develop low-cost housing, set up business enterprises, strengthen their political systems, and develop oil and other natural resources located on reservations. The ANA has by far the smallest budget of any of the 4 divisions of HDS, $29 million.

Administration on Aging (AoA)

The AoA was established under the Older Americans Act of 1965 to ensure that needy old people have sufficient food, money, and housing, and that the frail elderly have access to health care, transportation, and human contact. The AoA's primary duty is to administer grants to states, local governments, and Indian tribes for the operation of social-service programs for the aged. These programs provide old people with services in the home, such as home-delivered meals and homemaking assistance; services in the community, such as senior-center programs, adult day care, protection services, and legal and other counseling services; and access services, such as transportation to medical facilities, Social Security offices, and shopping areas. The AoA tries to guarantee that its funds are used for those elderly people in the greatest economic need and most at risk of losing their independence. In 1987, of the $724 million in grants the agency allotted, $422 million were spent on nutrition services, $270 million for supportive services, $7.5 million for nutrition and supportive services for Indian tribes, and $25 million for training, research, and special projects.

Administration on Developmental Disabilities (ADD)

The ADD was established in 1981 to promote self-sufficiency among the nation's approximately 4 million developmentally disabled and to help protect their legal rights. (As defined by the government, developmental disabilities are severe, chronic physical or mental impairments that manifest themselves before the age of 22.) The agency funds state programs that advocate the rights of disabled persons and provides grants for programs that make available an array of services. Such services run the gamut from prevention of disabilities to diagnosis, early intervention, therapy, education, training, employment, community living, and leisure opportunities. The agency also supports private and public programs that train people to work with the handicapped. In 1983, after Ronald Reagan proclaimed the 1980s the Decade of the Disabled, the agency launched a campaign to secure jobs for people with developmental disabilities. By 1987, 87,000 disabled men and women had been placed in positions in the private sector (outside of government), thereby saving the government $400 million in public-service payments.

Family Support Administration

The Family Support Administration (FSA) is the HHS's youngest division. It was established in 1986 by Secretary of Health and Human Services Otis R. Bowen, M.D., in his words, to "strengthen the family." It brought together programs that helped families in various ways: providing income subsidies, guaranteeing child support, settling refugee families, and assisting with home energy payments. Consolidation of these programs was aimed in part at increasing cooperation between them and giving states and interest groups a single, identifiable point of contact within HHS. But it was also intended to enable program directors to develop uniform strategies for reducing public dependency on the programs and thus reflected the Reagan administration's campaign to shrink the welfare state. In a sense, the FSA was created to hasten the demise of its components. Headed by the family support administrator, the FSA consists of four divisions: the Office of Family Assistance, the Office of Child Support Enforcement, the Office of Community Services, and the Office of Refugee Resettlement.

Office of Family Assistance

The Office of Family Assistance oversees Aid to Families with Dependent Children, a program that provides income support to needy families with children. The program is administered by the states, but the federal government, through the Office of Family Assistance, contributes part of the funding and establishes broad guidelines. To receive AFDC, a family must have at least 1 child under the age of 18 who is deprived of financial support because of the death, disability, or absence of 1 or both parents. In addition, the family must be impoverished, as defined by the state in which it resides. States also have the option of providing benefits to two-parent families in which the principal earner is unemployed. The size of the payments a family receives is determined by the state, on the basis of how poor it deems the family to be.

The AFDC program was established in 1935 as part of the public-assistance component of the Social Security Act. Since then, it has often been the target of reforms directed toward reducing administrative expenditures, combating embezzlement of funds by government employees, eliminating from its rolls "welfare cheats" (families who receive undeserved benefits by lying about their income), and discouraging families from separating in order to be eligible. In recent years, AFDC officials have provided job-training-and-placement services in an effort to reduce the number of people dependent on public assistance. Today, AFDC is the country's second largest public assistance program, after Supplemental Security Income. Together with SSI, food stamps, and unemployment compensation it constitutes what most people describe as "welfare." In the fiscal year 1986, an average of 3.7 million families received AFDC every month. Benefits for the year totaled $15.8 billion.

103

A Vietnamese refugee looks for a job with the assistance of a social worker from the U.S. Catholic Conference. The Office of Refugee Settlement funds public and private organizations that help immigrants adjust to life in the United States.

Office of Child Support Enforcement

By law, most parents who were once primary earners in their family but have since vacated the home, leaving children behind, are required to pay child support. According to the U.S. Bureau of the Census, there are today about 8.8 million households entitled to child support. However, only about 6 million receive some of what they are owed and only 4 million receive everything they are owed. Difficulty in collecting child-support payments is a continual headache for many families and is a primary cause of poverty for others. The Child Support Enforcement Program (CSE) has addressed this problem since 1975. This federal/state program helps parents secure child support in three main ways: by locating absent parents, by establishing *paternity* (identity of the father), and by obtaining court orders for payment. Although one of the primary goals of the program is to reduce the government's welfare bill by boosting the income of many single-parent families above the poverty line, all parents who are owed child support—not just those on welfare—are eligible to receive CSE services.

The Office of Child Support Enforcement represents the federal government in the CSE. It pays the states' administrative costs, issues guidelines, assists in location efforts, and works with the Internal Revenue Service (IRS) in calculating overdue child support using income tax returns. But states actually run the program. Under a 1984 bill, state agencies exercise extensive enforcement authority, including the power to withhold wages and to order courts to give priority to cases involving child support.

Office of Refugee Settlement

Since 1975, about a million refugees have settled in the United States, coming from such turbulent areas as Vietnam, Cambodia, Haiti, El Salvador, Cuba, and Afghanistan. Many have arrived here with little money, little knowledge of English, limited education, and few contacts. The Office of Refugee Settlement works with several other federal agencies to help refugees adjust to American society. The office's primary task is to administer grants that are used by states to provide refugees with medical care, financial assistance, education, and social services.

The office also helps states deal with the repercussions of the 1986 Immigration Reform and Control Act. Under this act, illegal aliens who had lived in the United States since 1982 were given the opportunity to become legal residents. By 1988, more than a million aliens had taken advantage of the

105

offer. This sudden increase in the number of people eligible for government services strained the financial resources of several states. To help the states provide public assistance, public health, and educational services to former aliens, the Office of Refugee Settlement now offers State Legalization Impact Assistance Grants.

Office of Community Services

The Office of Community Services administers Community Service Block Grants to states, territories, Indian tribes, and tribal organizations. These grants are used to pay for a wide variety of social-service programs for the poor. Local officials are given extensive powers to apportion the funds to ensure that money is applied where it is most needed at any given time. Social Services for which the grants are used include education, job training and placement, housing, health, emergency assistance, and income management. In fiscal year 1986, $350 million was distributed under this program.

The Office of Community Services also administers Low Income Home Energy Assistance Grants, which are used by states, territories, and tribal governments to assist low-income households in paying their energy bills and in refurbishing their home to make it more energy efficient. The sum of the energy assistance grant each state receives is determined by the amount of money its low-income residents spend annually on energy. In 1987, the program cost $1.8 billion and served 8.1 million households.

The Public Health Service

The mission of the Public Health Service (PHS) is "to promote the protection and advancement of the nation's physical and mental health."

The PHS is headed by the assistant secretary for health, who serves as the principal adviser to the HHS secretary on health and health-related matters. The assistant secretary is aided by the surgeon general, several deputy assistant secretaries, and the heads of the five PHS agencies. These agencies are the National Institutes of Health, the Food and Drug Administration, the Centers for Disease Control, the Alcohol, Drug Abuse, and Mental Health Administration, and the Health Resources and Services Administration.

The National Institutes of Health form one of the largest and most prestigious biomedical research centers in the world. It conducts research in its own laboratories, funds research by private institutions, provides grants for the training of researchers, and serves as a clearinghouse for information on the latest advances in medicine. It includes 12 national institutes that have specific research interests: the National Eye Institute; the National Institute on Aging; the National Cancer Institute; the National Heart, Lung, and Blood Institute; the National Institute of Diabetes and Digestive and Kidney Diseases;

A laboratory technician for the Food and Drug Administration (FDA). The FDA seeks to ensure that the nation's foods are pure, that drugs, biologic products, and therapeutic devices are safe, and that cosmetics are harmless.

the National Institute of Allergy and Infectious Diseases; the National Institute of Child Health and Human Development; the National Institute of Dental Research; the National Institute of Environmental Health Sciences; the National Institute of General Medical Sciences; the National Institute of Neurological and Communicative Disorders and Stroke; and the National Institute of Arthritis and Musculoskeletal and Skin Diseases.

The Food and Drug Administration attempts to ensure that the nation's food is safe, pure, and wholesome; that drugs, biologic products, and therapeutic devices for humans and animals are safe and effective; that cosmetics are harmless; and that electronic products do not expose users to dangerous amounts of radiation.

The Centers for Disease Control develop and conduct programs for disease prevention and control, environmental health, occupational safety and health, health promotion and education, and the training of health workers.

The Alcohol, Drug Abuse, and Mental Health Administration seeks to control and reduce alcohol abuse and alcoholism, drug abuse, and mental illness. It does so by conducting research in its laboratories and by funding research elsewhere in the country and around the world.

The Health Resources and Services Administration attempts to maintain and strengthen the supply, distribution, and utilization of health-care resources, and to ensure the delivery of health-care services to underserved populations. It has four divisions: the Bureau of Health Care Delivery and Assistance, the Bureau of Health Professions, the Bureau of Resources Development, and the Indian Health Service.

In addition to the five main divisions of the PHS, there are six staff offices within the Office of the Assistant Secretary for Health that perform management functions and administer additional programs. The National Center for Health Statistics collects and disseminates data on health in the United States and designs national data-collection systems. The President's Council on Physical Fitness and Sports attempts to improve physical fitness and health by promoting participation in exercise and sport by Americans of all ages. The Office of Population Affairs monitors population growth, conducts population research, and coordinates family planning programs.

Established in 1978, the National Toxicology Program coordinates research and conducts tests on toxic chemicals. The National Center for Health Services Research and Health Care Technology Assessment develops long-term strategies for health-care policy. The Office of Disease Prevention and Health Promotion spreads information on preventative health care.

In 1983, in Atlanta, doctors at the Centers for Disease Control (CDC), a branch of the PHS, isolated the virus that six years earlier had caused the mysterious death of several men attending an American Legion convention in Philadelphia.

Facilities

The secretary and other top officials of the HHS have their offices at the department's headquarters at 200 Independence Avenue SW, in Washington, D.C. But there are so many HHS employees that they all cannot possibly fit into one building. In fact they are scattered among thousands of facilities around the country. Many of the department's divisions and bureaus are not even headquartered in Washington, D.C. The main offices of the Public Health Service and those of three of its subdivisions—the FDA, the HRSA, and the ADAMHA—are located in Rockville, Maryland, just outside of Washington. Of the other two subdivisions of the PHS, the National Institutes of Health are located on a sprawling campus in Bethesda, Maryland, and the Centers for

HHS headquarters at 200 Independence Avenue SW in Washington, D.C., houses the offices of the department's secretary and other top officials. The majority of HHS's 120,000 employees work at facilities outside the nation's capital.

Disease Control are based in Atlanta, Georgia. The Social Security Administration has its headquarters in Baltimore, Maryland. Most of the work of the HCFA is done in Baltimore, although its top officials are in Washington. In fact, only two of the five operating divisions—HDS and the FSA—perform their major tasks in the nation's capital.

Many of HHS's operating divisions and subdivisions have their own networks of regional and local offices. For instance, the FDA has 6 regional field offices, 21 district offices, and 135 resident inspection posts (offices that handle investigations for areas that are a little larger than those covered by the district offices). The Social Security Administration alone maintains 6 program centers, 10 regional offices, and 1,300 local offices. HHS as a whole also operates 10 regional offices that handle relations with state and local governments, promote awareness of HHS programs in their areas, and provide administrative support to HHS programs that are operated on the community level. These regional offices are located in Boston, New York, Philadelphia, Atlanta, Chicago, Dallas, Kansas City, Denver, San Francisco, and Seattle.

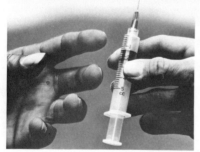

Posters distributed by HHS's National Institute of Drug Abuse dramatize the risks of contracting AIDS through drug use. As the AIDS epidemic grows, HHS will have to shoulder much of the burden for fighting the disease.

SEVEN

A Never-ending Struggle

O ver the years, HHS and its predecessors have done a great deal to improve the lives of Americans, particularly the needy. Social-insurance programs administered by the department have helped to protect countless aged, disabled, and unemployed workers against the hazards of unemployment. Supplemental Security Income and Aid to Families with Dependent Children have boosted millions of disadvantaged families, elderly poor people, and blind people over the poverty line. The department's many social-service programs have provided education, job training, counseling, and other assistance to a wide variety of groups, including refugees, runaway youths, the frail elderly, single parents, American Indians, the mentally retarded, and the disabled. The Public Health Service has helped expand the nation's network of hospitals, funded major medical research projects, protected consumers from hazardous foods and drugs, and combated epidemics of infectious diseases.

But HHS can by no means rest on its laurels, for there continue to be countless health and social-welfare problems that demand the department's attention. There are also numerous problems within HHS programs—particularly in the area of welfare—that must be addressed. In spite of decreasing unemployment during the 1980s, sociologist Michael Harrington's pessimistic description of the urban poor as a "hidden subculture . . . that perpetuated itself in an endless cycle" is perhaps more true today than during the 1960s when he wrote it. Though members of the upper and middle classes have benefited from the so-called economic boom of the Reagan era, most residents of ghettos have been left behind. As a result, disillusionment has become increasingly widespread, especially among poor youths. To attain a sense of belonging, an alarming number of impoverished youths have joined urban gangs.

The 1980s have also witnessed a startling rise in the number of homeless Americans. Many of the homeless hold jobs or are eligible to receive welfare benefits but simply cannot find homes they can afford. Others are victims of the limited coverage provided by federal welfare programs. Public assistance is currently available only to the blind, the disabled, the aged, and families with dependent children. Able-bodied childless workers between the ages of 18 and 65 who lose their job may receive unemployment compensation for as long as 26 weeks, but after that they are on their own. For people who are eligible for welfare, HHS programs provide too little incentive to work.

In the area of public health, HHS must soon deal with an AIDS crisis of major proportions. It is estimated that by 1991 the total number of AIDS cases reported since the beginning of the epidemic will have increased to 271,000. The price of providing health care to those suffering from the disease will have climbed to approximately $8 billion a year. HHS will have to help pay this massive bill, help find enough hospital beds to accommodate all the victims, and intensify the search for drugs to ensure that the epidemic does not continue indefinitely. The department must also take steps to limit the rise in health costs overall. Neither Medicare nor Medicaid can currently cover the exorbitant expense of extended hospital stays mandated by catastrophic illness or injury. Other major health-care problems that must be addressed include a nationwide shortage of nurses, the refusal by many hospitals to treat impoverished patients, and a major decline in the quality of nursing-home care brought on by rising costs, personnel shortages, and limits on federal spending for such facilities.

For most of his term in office, President Reagan paid little attention to these problems, instead concentrating on reducing funding for social programs and transferring programs to state and local governments. But in the last year of the Reagan presidency, there were indications that the pendulum might be swinging in the other direction—that after several years of cutting HHS programs, the administration, Congress, and HHS officials might be taking a renewed interest in spending money on social problems.

In the spring of 1988, with the president's blessing, the House and the Senate began work on a bill that would expand Medicare to include coverage for catastrophic illness. Under a proposal that emerged from a House-Senate

A 99-year-old woman and a 98-year-old man hold hands at an Alabama nursing home. One of the many challenges that HHS faces is trying to improve the quality of care in the nation's nursing homes, which have suffered in recent years from rising costs and personnel shortages.

conference and was signed into law by President Reagan, Medicare recipients, by paying an additional $4 a month in premiums and a 15 percent surcharge on income taxes, are eligible to receive the following: unlimited free hospital care after paying the first annual $564; unlimited free physician care after paying the first annual $1,370; 150 days a year of care in nursing homes; and 38 days a year of continuous home health care. Around the same time, the Senate began discussions on a bill that would overhaul the welfare system significantly for the first time since 1935. Because they observed that the existing system was no longer a source of temporary relief (as had originally been expected), but had become a way of life for its beneficiaries, senators proposed to transform AFDC from a public-assistance program to a jobs program. Sponsored by New York senator Daniel Patrick Moynihan, the bill would require states to provide education, training, and jobs to all able-bodied recipients of welfare except those with children under the age of three. In June 1988, HHS secretary Otis Bowen proposed regulations that would require hospitals with emergency rooms to examine all patients who seek treatment and to treat all those suffering medical emergencies and all women about to give birth, regardless of their ability to pay.

Will such efforts continue? It is impossible to say for sure. But one thing is certain: As long as poverty and public health problems continue to exist, HHS will play a critical role in assisting Americans in times of need.

Department of
Health and Human Services

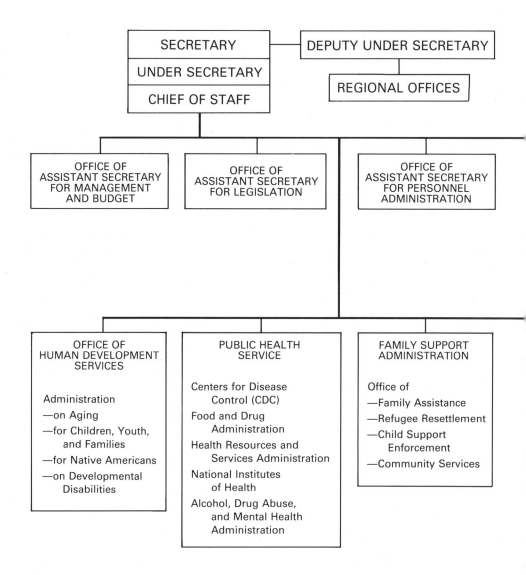

SECRETARY

UNDER SECRETARY

CHIEF OF STAFF

DEPUTY UNDER SECRETARY

REGIONAL OFFICES

OFFICE OF
ASSISTANT SECRETARY
FOR MANAGEMENT
AND BUDGET

OFFICE OF
ASSISTANT SECRETARY
FOR LEGISLATION

OFFICE OF
ASSISTANT SECRETARY
FOR PERSONNEL
ADMINISTRATION

OFFICE OF
HUMAN DEVELOPMENT
SERVICES

Administration

—on Aging

—for Children, Youth,
   and Families

—for Native Americans

—on Developmental
   Disabilities

PUBLIC HEALTH
SERVICE

Centers for Disease
   Control (CDC)

Food and Drug
   Administration

Health Resources and
   Services Administration

National Institutes
   of Health

Alcohol, Drug Abuse,
   and Mental Health
   Administration

FAMILY SUPPORT
ADMINISTRATION

Office of

—Family Assistance

—Refugee Resettlement

—Child Support
   Enforcement

—Community Services

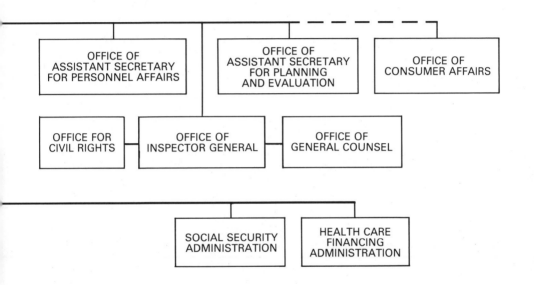

GLOSSARY

Aid to Families with Dependent Children (AFDC) A public-assistance program administered by HHS that provides income subsidies to poor one-parent families and some two-parent families in which the primary breadwinner is unemployed.

The Child Support Enforcement Program (CSE) A federal/state program that helps secure child support by locating absent parents, establishing paternity (identity of the father), and obtaining court orders for payment.

Food Stamp Program A public-assistance program that provides grocery coupons to low-income households to raise their "level of nutrition." It is administered by the Department of Agriculture and paid for out of general federal revenues.

Medicaid A federally funded, state-administered medical-insurance program for the poor, supervised by HHS.

Medicare A federal medical-insurance program for retired people covered by Social Security. It is funded by payroll taxes on employers and employees and is administered by HHS.

New Deal President Franklin D. Roosevelt's legislative and administrative program designed to promote economic recovery and social reform during the 1930s.

Old Age Survivors and Disability Insurance (OASDI) The official title for Social Security. It consists of retirement insurance, survivors' insurance, and disability insurance and is paid for by a payroll tax on employers and employees.

Operation Head Start A program supervised by the HHS's Administration for Children, Youth, and Families (ACYF) under which needy children receive education, health care, and counseling at centers around the nation.

Pension A sum paid regularly under given conditions to a person following his or her retirement from service or to his or her surviving dependents.

Supplemental Security Income A public assistance program administered by HHS that provides cash payments to the aged, the blind, and disabled people whose income is below a predetermined amount.

Unemployment Insurance A government insurance program supervised by the Department of Labor that makes weekly payments to workers who have been laid off and cannot find work. The insurance is paid for by taxes on employers.

SELECTED REFERENCES

Altmeyer, Arthur. *The Formative Years of Social Security.* Madison: University of Wisconsin Press, 1966.

Bell, Winifred. *Aid to Dependent Children.* New York: Columbia University Press, 1965.

Berkowitz, Edward, and Kim McQuaid. *Creating the Welfare State: The Political Economy of Twentieth Century Reform.* New York: Praeger, 1980.

Chen, Yung-Ping. *Social Security in a Changing Society.* Bryn Mawr, PA: McCahan Foundation, 1983.

Department of Health, Education, and Welfare. *A Common Thread of Service: A Historical Guide to the Department of Health, Education, and Welfare.* Washington, DC: HEW, 1970.

Derthick, Martha. *Policymaking for Social Security.* Washington, DC: Brookings Institution, 1979.

Leiby, James. *History of Social Welfare and Social Work in the United States, 1815–1972.* New York: Columbia University Press, 1978.

Miles, Rufus E., Jr. *The Department of Health, Education, and Welfare.* New York: Praeger Publishers, 1974.

Moynihan, Daniel Patrick. *The Politics of a Guaranteed Income.* New York: Random House, 1973.

Neal, Harry E. *Protectors: The Story of the Food and Drug Administration.* New York: Viking, 1970.

Patrick, William. *The Food and Drug Administration.* New York: Chelsea House Publishers, 1988.

Trattner, Walter I. *From Poor Law to Welfare State: A History of Welfare in America.* New York: Free Press, 1984.

Weicher, John C. *Maintaining the Safety Net: Income Redistribution Programs in the Reagan Administration.* Washington, DC: American Enterprise Institute, 1984.

Whitnah, Donald R., ed. *Government Agencies. Greenwood Encyclopedia of American Institutions.* Westport, CT: Greenwood Press, 1983.

Williams, Ralph C. *The United States Public Health Service, 1798–1950.* Richmond, VA: Whittet and Shepperson, 1951.

Witte, Edwin E. *The Development of the Social Security Act.* Madison: University of Wisconsin Press, 1962.

INDEX

Merle Broberg, now retired, was a professor of sociology at Bryn Mawr College from 1966 to 1985. He also served as assistant dean of Bryn Mawr's Graduate School of Social Work and Social Research for five years and as associate dean for three years. He holds a B.A. in anthropology from the University of Minnesota, an M.A. in social service from Bryn Mawr College, and a Ph.D. in sociology from the American University. He has written extensively on the issue of aging and has received grants from the McCahan Foundation, the Gerontological Society, and the Tokyo Metropolitan Institute of Gerontology. His previous books include *The Aging Veterans Population: Interorganizational Relations* and *Barbados* in the Chelsea House series PLACES AND PEOPLES OF THE WORLD. In 1981, he served as an adviser to the White House Conference on Aging. Before becoming a professor, he worked for many years as a social worker in the areas of child welfare, mental retardation, and low-income housing.

Arthur M. Schlesinger, jr., served in the White House as special assistant to Presidents Kennedy and Johnson. He is the author of numerous acclaimed works in American history and has twice been awarded the Pulitzer Prize. He taught history at Harvard College for many years and is currently Albert Schweitzer Professor of the Humanities at the City College of New York.